AF772530

INCULPABLE SIN

Albert V. Gallegos, Jr.

VANTAGE PRESS
New York / Los Angeles / Chicago

To those in whose memories
my son will live forever

FIRST EDITION

All rights reserved, including the right of
reproduction in whole or in part in any form.

Copyright © 1988 by Albert V. Gallegos, Jr.

Published by Vantage Press, Inc.
516 West 34th Street, New York, New York 10001

Manufactured in the United States of America
ISBN: 0-533-07847-4

Library of Congress Catalog Card No.: 87-90316

CONTENTS

I
The Incident

Ten days had expired after we buried our seventeen-year-old son, Albert III, when I endeavored to indite this soulful book, addressing the unutterable devastating horror that totally consumed us with the bitter taste of death. His death, which will possess our consciousness of life as a dull lethargic condition until our deaths supervene, was on a Monday, February 28, 1983, at 5:36 P.M.

It was far and beyond the comprehensive powers of our minds to conceive what exasperated him to his hideous madness, leaving behind the total environment of decadence with a trail of solemn hearts. Without deliberation and suspicion, hastily resolving his uncalculated and impulsive problem, he committed what society condemns as an iniquitous deed of mankind—suicide. Even in the extremity of our insanity, possessing our mental facilities with the concept of total annihilation, my wife and I could not give countenance to our son's act.

Under this inconceivable and detestable circumstance, a seemingly eternal period of perpetual agony, our strength consolidated, we sought, amid our desperate and despairing cries, answers to some baffling questions. Why did it happen? Why us? Why not somebody else? What could we have done to prevent his death? Where did we go wrong? Could the availability of materialistic offerings have altered the end result? In my devastation, submerged in my complete misery, I ventured a wretched thought of what despicable sin I had irrecoverably committed to be bequeathed such a tragedy. In my inquiry, beset by a cluster of pleading questions, not even in a well-contrived investigation did I encounter any answers. The aggregate of my endeavors was a unanimous defeat, where the sovereign power of death was triumphant. I never envisioned, scrutinizing the private domain of my perception, the horrid destiny that has pertinaciously enervated my life.

In the privacy of my thoughts I cannot think for the cry of my eternal agony, and in the solitude of my sleep I cannot rest for the memory of my son. Ferocity of despair arrested our actions with a profound sentiment of unusual animosity, disastrously exposing an obscure idiosyncracy from the bottom of our hearts. In the extreme of this ghastly horror, haunting us day and night obstinately, how is it possible to survive? The scar of death, the miserable wound so deeply penetrated in the entity of our existence, will linger on, enduring until the treatment of time heals our wounds. Our disorganized hearts, affected wholeheartedly by the loss of our son, have been subjugated, collapsing into a state of insensitivity. We have become inconsistent with our passions, lacking the necessary power to penetrate the thicket of our agony. Total decimation of memory is beyond the accessible powers of the mind. In the midst of the insurmountable suffering, engaging my thoughts with my son's calamitous death, I concluded personally with an unbounded conception that if a terminal illness had befallen our son, his death would have been confronted with reluctant harmony. But the sudden shock, hearing the information of the shuddering horror, an expression outside the grace of God, sufficed to distort the permanence of my stability. The agony of that split second is indescribable and beyond the comprehension of the mind.

Various laconic writers and terse psychometricians, succinctly mastering the intricacies of penmanship and perplexities of mind, respectively, have effectively analyzed the particulars of grief, rendering considerable light to minimize a lingering pain. What prompted me to invade the privacy of my thoughts, disturbing the agitation of mind and spirit, was the unfathomable affection toward my son and a desire to unfold the memory, adducing the emotions of unaccountable capacity, of an overwhelming experience. As I pen my mournful story, consumed with this languishing sorrow, I weep profusely, shedding tears while expounding on the details of this lamentable tribulation. It is my intention, hopefully, signifying a course of action that I propose to follow, captivated in the primary object of my literature, to alleviate my perpetual grief. We possess the capacity to drown ourselves in our grief, depending on the intensity of our feelings. Fighting ferociously from expediting matters, from reaching that point of consumption, I have concentrated my energies, physically and mentally, to escape the indignity of falling into that pitiable state of total destruction.

In my solitary moments of the nights, as I disturb the memory of my grief and stir the poignant sense of loss of my son, the ordinary powers of my mind recollect the anomalous absence of the instinctive ability to cry. I endeavored to cry during the atmosphere of death, but my eyes rendered futile efforts. I delved into the profundity of my subconsciousness, which, conditioned through the process of a repressive cuture, had hollowed out the tears of my heart. I come from a race noted for their valor and their grace of manhood, deriving our principal source of pleasure from it. The earliest recollection of my youth is embodied with this conception. At the time my son succumbed to the temptation of death, I was possessed by this mode of life, alienated from tears, a victim of an insensitive environment. But the mournful influence and the horror of the occasion violently apprehended the force of my feelings, moving vehemently into the private chambers of my heart to free my tears. Without a doubt I grew insensible to pain. You may fancy me mad when I vociferate that any deplorable crisis is more tolerable than this tragedy. In the present state of my condition I now cry freely, my tears steadily increasing at the mental image of my son.

In our bereavement, incapacitated by the sacred thoughts of our son during our individual meditation, the immediate family and the legion of friends were everlastingly compassionate, constantly attenuating the surroundings of death with their sympathy. Their commiseration was a faithful struggle to succor us from our incoherence. The encumbrance, inordinately displaying itself in a host of sporadic sensations and too wearisome to endure, lay scattered about our minds and bodies so that only God knew the nature of our malady.

It is thus, dreading the shuddering result of my past event, functioning amid this intolerable agitation of spirit, and abhorring the absolute effect that afflicts the morale of my existence, that I venture forth to document the privacy of my thoughts for this book. My arduous effort, nevertheless, as I propose to myself, enchained by the influence of my son's death, will afford me the endeavor to immortalize him, patronizing myself through all subsequent time on this earth. I will not forbear from portraying in words the merits of my case, pledging that my son's inopportune death will not be in vain.

Our friends, incorporating a conglomeration of activities, for it was thought proper to influence our minds with ease, faithfully suggested innovative methods of forgetting. Creativity, they said, is a method of oblivion. I would be an ingrate, an ungrateful villain, if I did not take heed of the healthy solicitude with which our friends attended to our needs. But I don't want to forget my son. As the opportunity presents itself during the course of each day, I cannot help thinking of him, becoming intoxicated with the wonder of his image. My wife and I conceived a wonderful boy, ecstatically affecting the emotions of our existence. His death disintegrated the emotions into a wasteland, lacking liveliness, interest, and humor. The barren surfaces of our souls reflect an image of loneliness, emptiness, and desolation. In my attempt to pursue any activity my laborious efforts are permeated with the thoughts of my son, inevitably consuming me with the reality of life. Our eternal suffering has annihilated all the vigor in our hearts and vitality of our lives. As I betake myself reluctantly to the atmosphere of this composition, laboring incessantly day and night, I become frantically wearied and enormously sad. I struggle on occasions, especially when his memory presents itself as impalpable shadows, to maintain my composure internally. My appearance is only one of disguise, playing a role in life where my act is performed unwillingly.

It is now rendered mandatory, employing with dexterity the vernacular and literary language that I possess, to acquaint you with the harsh facts that will emphatically unfold the imprudent and deliberate destruction. My knowledge of the evidence, having examined it thoroughly, affords me the occasion to delineate the circumstances of my son's dreadful death.

My observation of that consequential day, as it brings at once to my mind the last occasion on which I visualized my son alive, necessitates much reflection. I endeavor, as such turbulent thoughts pervade my mind, relapsing my mental facilities to the bosom of agonizing memories of my beloved, to embellish a descriptive analysis of the unspeakable horror of that day. It was hot for a winter day in February. A major portion of that fateful day was commencing to wear away as I prepared to take leave of a lecture at college. As the latter part of that day descended upon us, my son and I engaged in a rather simple discourse concerning his anticipation of a telephone call concerning a job. During his brief monologue I expressed my entire confidence in him, which elicited an enthusiastic facial expression that particularly arrested my unanimous attention. While he proceeded to enchant me with his conversation, lending beauty to the essence of the dialogue, I whimsically perceived another demonstration of jubilance in his appearance, which, possessing both hearts, his and mine, sealed an everlasting inspiration with the warmest ardor in my heart. My son had recently resolved to divorce himself from school because of tedium, collecting all his energies to strengthen his mental capacity to acquire a General Equivalence Diploma. (G.E.D.) I had initially become seriously alarmed for some possible negative consequences, as I could not help thinking it my duty to discourage him. My remonstration was in vain. He had no wish for my advice, but was impregnating his mind with the concept of finding work. He had temporarily entertained the idea of supporting himself as an enlisted man in pursuance of his duty. At length, as I conditioned myself to depart after our colloquy, it was there, indeed, the last occasion that I consecrated my entire vision on him alive, concluding with a mere good-bye. His attitude seemed positive, expressing an appearance of satisfaction through his jovial mood. Never was there a trace or any indication of the malignant danger that was to prevail.

I was at college when our oldest daughter, Gina,

tainted my lecture with the shuddering terror that had befallen her brother. My mood faded into horror, my heart melted into insanity, and my nature vanished into obscurity. I was in shock! I was besieged with every quality of dizziness, as the all-absorbing atmosphere suffocated the aptitude of my mind to the rank of inferiority. I was at a loss to comprehend what wretched motive had traversed his path of hostility. I was seized by an uncontrollable desire for God at that moment, enunciating the following disturbing expression from the bottom of my heart. I remonstrated, "Oh, God, please, God, don't let it happen—any horror but this!" A suffocating lump confined itself firmly and deeply in the vicinity of my esophagus and windpipe so that I couldn't breathe. All was now in a state of confusion and despair—but efforts were constantly made to find the sympathy of God. Several circumstances occurred immediately. I fought to regain myself, my stern composure, but failed. Because of the extremity of the matter at hand, I drove in a state of incoherence to the hospital. In the annals of driving, rendering it evident after a careful investigation, nobody could have surpassed my velocity of rapid impetuosity that was attained in the extremity of my absolute woe. To all appearances, as it was beyond evidence, I drove safely enough to avoid another drastic consequence. In the midst of all my suffering, I prayed in murmuring sounds en route to my destination. I selfishly pleaded with God, bargaining for my son's life. At length I terminated my prayer, an earnest appeal, by resigning myself to God's will and by placing my son's life in his hands.

In spite of my inconceivable rapidity, I could not best the incessant principle of time or the unconquerable element of death. I arrived at the hospital and, without hesitation, rushed hurriedly to the emergency room. As I proceeded insanely to converge with my son's destiny, my eyes lamentably perceived my wife's discernible expression. I immediately calculated with a nervous anxiety that our son was dead. My perception, accompanied with a sensation of fear, was not incorrect. Her initial utterance, as she fought the excessive expression of tears, was, "He's gone."

The uproar that ensued, an explosion of human indignity rendered impulsively, is beyond the total comprehension of any mental capacity. No person, orator or writer, filled with the characteristics of earthly ingenuity is sufficiently qualified to convey my indescribable human sensations in concise oral discourse, or in a pithy written composition. As I reflect upon the scene, keeping in mind the struggle of so violent a nature, bewildering, and so enduring to paralyze the whole life of a single individual, I sobbed, screaming and yelling, "Oh, God, not my son, not my son. Why, dear God? Why? Haven't I served you well?" The force of my clamor, a vehement expression of anguish and protest, from earth to heaven, pierced the heart of the sanctuary of God. My mental and physical endowments were lapsed into a state of insensitivity. I was totally confounded.

A sense of indignation that degraded the character of my soul instituted the seed of rebellion against God. The convulsion of my anger was emphatically directed at God for taking my son away. In our serene composition of life we never contemplated the possibility of being vulnerable to such imprudence of life. Fate commanded it, and it happened. Destiny contrived the bitter plan. My confusion and animosity provided me the insipience to impute the blame for my son's action to the Almighty. The assembly of friends sharing our deep mourning, displaying commendable prudence, and unfurling marvelous words of wisdom, brought it to my attention, appealing to my principles of reasoning, saying that God works in mysterious ways. During the atmosphere of decadence, a period deteriorating my presence of mind, I did not succumb to persuasion. I was so overwhelmed with my invective against God that the foundation of my countenance, the real character of my personage, was thrust into a state of hostility. There was a hidden power, an unknown spirit in me, that maneuvered my mental faculties instinctively through the elements of shock, disbelief, and anger before I saturated my mind with the displeasing conclusion that my son was dead.

Without reservations I am constrained to betray, standing so well in the patterns of personal experience, my confidential thoughts that have ensconced themselves safely in the private chambers of my brain. The specific account of the scene that transpired next, vivifying passages of description with the precise mastery of words in my vocbulary, is the most peculiar sequence of events ever adduced from an unexpected tempest of death. As I regretfully directed my walk toward the immediate vicinity where my son reposed, the constitution of my mouth desiccated in the extreme, the temperature gradient of my hands degenerated beyond the phenomenon of cryogenics, the weight of my legs gravitated toward the base of the earth, and the intrinsic properties of my life dwindled into the vortex of oblivion. The gravest necessity that apprehended my reasoning, employing my mental process to draw the following conclusion, was to see and touch my son with a commanding sense of closure. So potent was the effect of the circumstances that I quivered unwillingly at the petulant moment that tortured my nerves. I stood in consternation and absorbed in contemplation. The thought of my own death traversed my mind, inebriating the sober balance of my stance. My vision was riveted upon my son with a profound and most reverent awe, as I touched his face and kissed him for the last time. My soul grew bitter with the heart of a demon, cursing the day, because in my dreadful spirit and shrunk sensation, I knew that the opportunity would never present ittself to relish the effects of his inspiration. I confess wholeheartedly the impossibility of kissing my son appropriately due to the process of an initially inadequate condition within my culture where men are unaccustomed to exhibit affection publicly toward other men. Men are contaminated by this quality of behavior, a firm conviction ingrained in their youth, and I, seeking to satisfy my inquisitive mind, will affirm in an unofficial capacity the undeniable fact. And now I grieve to the soul, being much affected by the frigidity of my culture.

That night, the day of our son's death, my wife and I, amidst our infinite misery and attempting to search out the ultimate truth, found it compulsory to examine, demanding complete satisfaction to appease our souls, the anomalous and deplorable phenomenon. Nevertheless, we had to achieve a state of cognizance of the ghastly incident. We began piecing together the mystification of that day. My wife and our oldest daughter, Gina, were leisurely watching television that afternoon. Tina, our youngest daughter, was displaying her exploits in volleyball at school, while Albert was in the process of dispersing his amiable fellowship at the house of Laura, his girl friend. Then the most befuddled scene was about to ensue. Albert scampered into the house in a manner that absolutely exhibited anger, educed entirely by his facial expression. As he made his entrance, it became evident that he had been involved in an undesirable predicament with Laura. In the midst of his unrestraining rush, my wife managed to inject a question. He replied, "No," to the question in an unsuitable and inappropriate sound and then proceeded into our bedroom. Albert's acrimonious answer did not arrest my wife's attention, nor did it prompt her immediately to explore his raging mood. She never envisioned Albert would be so agitated to the point of self-destruction. The unexpected or sudden termination of life had never, even in thought or jest, been ingrained in our minds. Then suddenly, a few seconds afterward, there was a sound resembling that of a firecracker, accompanied simultaneously with a dolorous yell. My wife became bewildered and entangled with her thoughts. She sped in an incalculable velocity to investigate that alarming and ghastly sound. As she arrived frantically at our bedroom with a hesitant mind and uncertain heart, she penetrated the unpalatable and distasteful atmosphere only to discern the most appalling and unfathomable scene any mother could experience. Her primary visualization was that of our son lying in a supine dorsal position in dormancy. Without any hesitation, being cognizant of the calamity, she immediately administered mouth-to-mouth resuscitation. Of all the extreme, unfortunate, and painful experiences, none is more agonizing, mentally or physically, than the unrelenting struggle of a mother attempting desperately and impetuously to save her dying child. As my wife held our son in her arms, close to her bosom, he was still conscious. There remained a trace of life by the grace of God. Placing her hand near the proximity of his chest, she came upon the gruesome realization that a bullet, fired from my pistol, had pierced the heart.

Determined and fighting madly to keep Albert alive, and with her inherent quest for the truth, she whispered distinctly in his ear for the ruthless and disturbing motive that drove him to his evil insanity. "Why did you do it,

Son? Why? Your father and I love you very much," she told him mournfully while he remained lethargic for a few seconds, with a dim consciousness of life.

He acknowledged in a trembling, quavering voice, "Laura left me, Mom, and I love her." The tone of his voice, totally uprooting the core of my wife's soul, will forever echo in my wife's mind, reflecting sound waves of despair. As he appeared to be getting weaker and weaker and nearer to death, my wife poured all her living breath into him. She sustained the ventilation of her living breath until the Emergency Medical Service (E.M.S.) arrived at the house. My wife resolved in her mind to inform our son that we loved him very much, making these the last words of affection that she would say to him. The splendid, extraordinary courage my wife produced under this fierce and violent pandemonium is beyond the best of mortals. Nevertheless, morally and physically, her acts were absolutely useless and without effect. We had just received a terrible beating, my wife and I. He who was the first fulfilment in our lives, who had engendered complete awe in us, and who had perpetually inspired us with his love was now the reliable source of pain in our hearts.

The E.M.S. was irrefutably swift and irrefragably prompt in its arrival at the scene of catastrophe. It must have been five minutes after the disaster, as my wife was deeply absorbed in the scenery of death, that her hopes reached the summit of gratification with the arrival of the ambulance. Because of the intense nature of the case, a Catholic priest, Father Mitchell, accompanied the ambulance, providing the spiritual comfort my wife needed amid the appalling and intolerable horror. It was the primary task of the ambulance technicians, discharging the onerous duties of their profession, to stabilize Albert's vital signs before engaging in the expedition to the hospital. While the technicians attempted to succeed perfectly well in their endeavors, my wife stood vigilantly, praying incessantly to God to consider our son's faculties and impulses and the salvation of his soul. She endeavored tenaciously, extending the rigor of her determination, to make herself available during the intense ordeal. She grew pale as the intensity of despair increased with every dying second that was gradually ticking away into the past. At length it became absolutely conspicuous to Father Mitchell, utilizing the least effort of his mental powers, or to any other human perception that was overwhelmed by the appearance of death that Albert's fate was undoubtedly in the hands of God. Father Mitchell mentally concluded that a fatal consequence was inevitable. The damage done was too extensive internally so that the facts were altogether too convincing and too damning to overcome. At this juncture, Father Mitchell, hesitating no longer, prepared the final absolution ceremony for our son. Much to the astonishment of everyone present, Albert seemed to revive at different moments from his deep sleep, only to render false illusions of life on each occasion. The excessive warmth of Father Mitchell's sympathy, presented during the entire period of need, will never be forgotten. My heart is filled with the sincerest affection, an intensification of profound gratification, to know that my son was conscious when he received the last sacrament. The acknowledgment of his death was purposely prolonged through the quality of precious time generously extended by God. For my part I am totally convinced, adhering to my faith in Christ, that my son is in Heaven. I will sum up, using but a few words, what constitutes the essence of my story. There is no medicine in the world that is potent enough to save our souls other than that of our Savior, Jesus Christ, our Lord.

II
The Aftereffect

The light of each day will not reach its dying moment without me nurturing my most sacred memories of my son. In the privacy of my thoughts a string of ever-remembered occasions always affect my thinking efforts, immediately recalling to the surface of my memory former activities in which Albert and I engaged. While occupied with these thoughts, my moments are filled with only the noble qualities of contentment. Every day when I busy myself with the different daydreams respecting Albert, I find comfort, rejoicing in the midst of each purifying effect that seemingly appears to overcome the dreary solitude of my life. In such a state of mind I am always led away by my feelings while my mind is marked with pits of recollection. The constant association of certain particulars impels me to create imagerial impressions in my mind, enkindling the very depth of my soul with a happiness to wonder. As the light of the day comes to a close with the birth of night and I recline my head on the pillow anticipating sleep, my consciousness, which masters my power of thinking, directs my unanimous thoughts to one mental influence, my son. While in the deep possession of my dreams, an image of my son evolves like a shadow amid a dim mist, always flowing gingerly about the earth. My state of mind renders me the opportunity to glance into his eyes as he walks toward me, displaying the most favorable disposition with his smile and his jovial mood. The soft caress of the breeze presents a soothing touch to his face. I find myself paralyzed, lacking the power to touch him. I endeavor to utilize the most aggressive powers the heart can produce to communicate with him, but to no avail, rendering me insensible at once. My summons, a dogged obstinacy with which I persisted in my dream, is unheard by Albert. I venture out to arrest his attention by standing before him with a heart characterized by wild excitement, but his eyes fail to capture the path of my potent vision. My arduous endeavor, distinguished by intensity of feeling, is to gradually embrace and successfully comfort him. But I can't. His beloved eyes do not offer the recognition that would completely satisfy my pleasing fancy, consequently bringing about an air of deep solemnity to my heart. I do not content myself with this encounter, but its efect environs my dream with unceasing gloom. Just the expression of his smile is sufficient to emit the inherent luster of his countenance. The common denominator of my dream is the consciousness of death. Then I notice myself, my original self, inexpressibly enervated by the agony of my dream, as if through an extensive period of inanition. I struggle to reorganize my senses, the ordinary powers of mind, and endeavor to evaluate my real condition. The intensity of my dream seems to oppress and stifle me. Still possessed by the quality of my dream, I lie quietly and continue to make the mental energy exercise my reason. The atmosphere, contaminated with the disorder of my dream, becomes intolerably insuperable. The vision of my eyes is obstructed by the sudden gush of tears that flow incessantly because, at length, I am deprived of the sacred privilege of embracing my son. Then, while still in the dreamy sensation pervading my frame of mind, I hear his voice, compelling me to shed more irrepressible tears. As I stretch out my arms to confine his soul with mine, attempting to vociferate my unfathomable love for him, I awake to confront reality, which environs me with sadness in my heart, tears in my eyes, and emptiness in my soul. To console myself in my torment I pray, entering into a spiritual communion with God to supplicate God for a blessing of peace, comfort, and meaning.

Throughout the movement of the day, miserable as I am, in a low, quivering cry I petitioned God to overcome this utterly unanticipated calamity. There hangs a cloud of intense sorrow, an incarnate horror that only God could alleviate, incumbent eternally upon my life. Beneath the pressure of horror such as this, the surviving trace of good within me succumbed. The moodiness of my composure has increased to hatred of almost anything that presents itself within the premise of my temperament. It was beyond the perimeter of destiny to humbly beg God to shield me from the terror at hand, for my pitiable calamity had already crossed beyond the threshold of salvation. But in spite of a sustained bombardment of pain, my faith was unwavering and I besought God to walk with me during my time of tribulation. I prayed more vigorously than before for a blissful sense of relief and a future felicity for my family. It was suggested, providing a rendition of a learned imagination, that God forbids suffering that exceeds a person's endurance. I, without initiating defiance to anybody or anything like explanation, confess that this undue tragedy of such propensity will suffice forever in my lifetime.

During the funeral services, while I was buried in the gloom of my own heart and compulsively dependent on the most intense and solemn meditation, a gracious person attracted my undivided attention by handing me a card with a message inscribed on it titled "Footprints." Through the medium of my disturbed vision, my eyes quaintly endeavored to particularly exercise themselves with the inscription that became the essence of my attention. The scrutiny of the engraving, as I now call to mind the misty influence of that bitterly lamenting condition that caused an icy chill through my whole body, had sufficed to register itself upon my memory. The card was written anonymously and reads as follows:

One night a man had a dream. He dreamed he was walking along the beach with the LORD. Across the sky flashed scenes from his life. For each scene, he noticed two sets of footprints in the sand; one belonging to him, and the other to the LORD.

When the last scene of his life flashed before him, he looked back at the footprints in the sand. He noticed that many times along the path of his life there was only one set of footprints. He also noticed that it happened at the very lowest and saddest times in his life.

This really bothered him and he questioned the LORD about it. "LORD, you said that once I decided to follow you, you'd walk with me all the way. But I have noticed that during the most troublesome times in my ilfe, there is only one set of footprints. I don't understand why when I needed you most you would leave me."

The LORD replied, "My precious, precious child, I love you and I would never leave you. During your times of trial and suffering, when you see only one set of footprints, it was then that I carried you."

My wife had recently concentrated her efforts on the pleasurable interest of penmanship, communicating admirably with each member of the family through this innovative method. Because of our hasty life-style, each of us had strayed carelessly through life with no thought of each other, forcing my wife to thoroughly entertain us with her writing efforts, which would be fully appreciated in our solitude. Albert had enveloped his sustenance of life with a considerable increase of remoteness, lacking warmth and friendliness within the neighborhood of the family. Indeed, to judge from the progression of life-styles from the remaining members of the family, respectively, strange as it may seem, it is fair to infer guilt of gross negligence amongst ourselves. It was now very distinct, as I was inclined to believe, the direction we all had hitherto taken. This circumstance did not fail to appropriate for us the occasion, the ultimate success, to approach Albert about his immediate plans in life. Some were moments that, I am willing to confess, rendered no disquietude to us, finding full confidence in the efficiency of our conversations.

My wife, with the best heart in mind—but then that is part of her nature—penned a high-spirited letter to Albert on January 31, offering a sense of understanding for some wretched moments of his life and compassion for any discomfort that might beset him. In her heart she wished for nothing more ardently than his happiness. The letter, all the time at her command, complying with her own prudence for the justifiable moment of delivery, never reached its destiny. As fate would have it, Albert died during that lapse of time. She never committed herself to releasing the letter, finding difficult to contrive a method at the proper moment for so doing. The bitter taste of death that pervaded her soul left her in a contrite spirit. At length, we encouraged ourselves to display the letter, pinning it inside the opened casket, perhaps as a testimony of regret with a superior sensitivity of feeling. The letter was deliberately entombed with Albert, irrevocably affixing a seal to everything physically associated with him, excluding his memory, which will forever flourish supremely in our hearts. But the human condition of my heart supplied me the hindsight to pen the letter in duplicate. It would be quite unacountable, impossible to conceive, how anything related to the death of a loved one could have escaped the archives of our memory. Nevertheless, however unpleasant, I will familiarize you with my wife's document as a reminder of an unforeseen evil that to this day is in no danger of reprieving itself. I endeavor to maintain my spirit, struggle from within to elicit courage, and refrain from bursting into tears at each reading of the letter that hosts an undertaking of great difficulty. The letter is imbued with clarity and reads as follows:

Dear Albert, *January 31st, 1983*
One day you will inherit a love of life—right now I know you feel confused, and maybe, I guess, scared of the future. I feel guilty—yes, and bad. I wish I could have taken all your pains away when you were hurt and sad. This is one wish I guess God could not grant me—that you would not suffer so.

The day you were born was the happiest day of my life. When you are a man and out on your own remember to keep a giving heart and to be sincere. Never envy what others have but be thankful for what God gives you—health, beauty, and love.

You are already very blessed. Others always love you. Be good to yourself and work hard. The things your heart desires are going to be that much better if you have worked hard to (achieve) get them. Be good to the girl that will be your wife. Remember, your mother was a young girl once. God is by your side.

Love,
Mom

Within the range of my mental powers, I am relentlessly haunted, day and night, by the cogitation of what seems to be a cogent question. Could good fortune have prevailed and aided us in some measure had Albert's eyes fallen upon the letter in his solitude? This question dwells in my mind, murmuring sounds of sorrow under my breath. It is utterly impossible, beyond the perimeter of words, to contrive a laconic style of expression to explicate the tormenting distress of mind that arises from this letter. We are left with a deep and an unaccountable sentiment of grief. The remaining days of our lives shall be filled with sorrow, a sorrow with an everlasting impression, enduring until the roots of our lives no longer sustain the wealth of life itself. Although the days of our happiness are over, as we sadly lament our fallen son, our thoughts, entombed in the memory of our hearts, fall back on the eternal love for him to overcome this overwhelming desolation. During the prettiest days of the year, which produce consuming memories, as I venture into the privacy of my thoughts, I am possessed with a burning obsession for him that I cannot quench. It is a particular feeling that remains anonymous in my soul, wrapped up in a sense of divinity, mirroring the nature of God. During the dismal days of my life marked by gloom that cannot be transmitted by words to the multitude, though I don't fail to make the endeavor, an icy chill possesses my body, freezing me to the bones. As I conceive the immedicable effects of the action of my senses, I ponder upon my own destiny, hovering between tears and sorrow each day of my life. Anxiety oppresses me, costing a perpetual struggle that has become an abstraction of my constitution. The complexity of my demeanor, touching my sanity to suggest excessive sentimentality, is decaying the resoluteness of my endurance. As days of bitter grief have elapsed, but I still managed to survive, a conspicuous change has come over the features of my mental faculties. My ordinary self has been greatly altered, swept by the velocity of the horror. As the whole of day pours forth upon the vagueness of night, it transmits waves of unceasing gloom. I perceive clearly the dreams of agitation that await me each night as I lie down to sleep.

A possessing sleep consumes me—a sleep like that of death. And then very suddenly there come back to my soul the shadows of memory that present once again the wearisomeness of their effects. As I continue deep into my somnolence, my mind somnambulates within the compass of the written words of my wife's letter, which, solidly cemented in the repertoire of my memory, provide the accommodation for my sleep each night.

III
Faith

With some deliberate air of forethought, after the death of my son, as I found myself to be thoroughly broken down, it became totally necessary to assume an investigation of my shattered faith in God. A bitter impulse in my heart had begun to imperil my soul with a primitive pulsation of hating power that is found in the vilest character that directs cruel men in the world. I was committing sin, swallowed in an equivocal spirit of meaness. At length, after a period when such inconsistencies of thought had most fully pervaded my mind, my inquisitive endeavors enkindled the fire of my faith, strengthening my soul and spirit thenceforth. The rejuvenation of faith excited my curiosity to seek much comfort in the Bible.

Faith, in a general sense, I see examining the particular definition from the dictionary, means to believe in the word of someone. Theological faith is the adherence of the intellect, under the influence of grace, to a revealed truth, not only because of its intrinsic evidence, but because of the authority of God revealing it. Faith is the anticipated reality of what we hope for, the demonstrative proof of what the mind does not see. Thus it is said that faith is obscure, but infinitely superior to all human knowledge in stability and certainty, since it is based on God Himself, infinite and infallible Truth, who can neither deceive nor be deceived.

My own heart can detail with awe the intensity of gratification derived from faith. To those who embrace faith I need not burden myself elucidating the nature of tranquility thus derived. Faith is future life. At first I could not understand my detestable thoughts—but soon my endeavors were to get the better of the apathy that had come over me. Faith has prevented the destruction that occupied my mind in such extremity. My principal grief was diminished in the bliss of God's power. The frightening sensation that unmanned me at first, as I now suppose, was the complete loss of hope that strung my nerves unconditionally.

In the tempestuous history of mankind legions of pious people have encountered instant destruction because of faith. Amid the intensity of terror, no one will ever know the agony within their souls at the moment of doom. The attempts to account for their tenacity, absorbed in the perfected knowledge of the Bible, give rise to the purity of the strength of faith. The strength of a vitally important quality will soon penetrate the hearts of even the strongest adherent to any philosophical school of skepticism. The exceeding majesty of faith is thoroughly exemplified in the Book of Judges, which, accompanied by the inspiration of other virtues, also acknowledges the omnipresent quality of truth. I need not remind you that, apart from this consideration, from the long and extensive catalog of human history, the possibilities of other abundantly supplied selections with essential specimens of faith were superfluous, exceeding the simple examples that came to mind in the course of my composition, which so vividly impressed my fancy.

The Book of Judges, with specific themes of faith in which the interest is all-consuming, renders evidence, through the delineation of historical records, of twelve heroes of Israel whose outstanding battles and tremendous accomplishments against the enemy enabled them to free the people of God. God, because of various well-authenticated circumstances, would inflict punishment on the people of Israel because of their disobedience and loss of faith in him. Eventually, nevertheless, the people of Israel would fall into a hopeless state of oppression, ruled by the evident terror of pagan nations. At length, after much suffering during the long lapse of years and thronged by the people's repentant asseverations, God would deliver them, dispatching military heroes (synonomous with Judges) to conquer the enemy.

The most famous Judge, whose whimsical nature exemplifies faith, satisfying his sentiment, both his mental power and physical strength, which arose from his bosom for God, is the immensely important character of Samson. Samson, becoming the source of numerous unpleasant military endeavors toward the Philistines and heavenly vested with full powers that were beyond the comprehension of the ordinary mind, was from the clan of the Danites. The Israelites had offended God, who therefore delivered them to the Philistines for forty years. Samson judged Israel for twenty years in the days of the enemy. Then, as Samson's fate began to unfold before his people, he fell in love with a woman in the Wadi Sorek whose name was Delilah, impairing his mortal condition through his human sensations. She beguiled him, extracting the secret of this great strength, which was his hair. Delilah proceeded to shave Samson's hair and sold him to the Philistines for eleven hundred shekels of silver. Samson, endeavoring to escape, was useless for all purposes of vitality, realizing that God had abandoned him for disobeying. It was arranged among the leaders of the Philistines, enchancing their advantage over Samson, especially under the circumstances, to gouge his eyes out. The Philistines found blindness the most effectual process in subduing Samson, leaving him in a living agony like death. This condition was nearly unaltered until the lords of the Philistines were evidently influenced to sacrifice him to their god Dagon, proceeding without hesitation to pull Samson from the grinding stone to amuse them. By this time Samson's faith had harvested the fruits of his labor, seasoning his strength to destroy the enemy of God. The Philistines thronged the temple, about three thousand, when Samson, playing the part of a buffoon, rested his hands in a seemingly easy position between the columns that supported the temple. The curiosity of the throng was excited as Samson, determined to hazard a praying effort to God, pleaded for forgiveness and to be remembered again. His intentions, from a divine influence that operated in him to inspire virtue, were to die willingly with the enemy to avenge himself for the loss of his eyes and to please God. With a perceptible effort induced by God, Samson's prayer became a reality. An exaggeration of strength diffused through every part of Samson's frame, and with the fullest exertion of power he disintegrated the stone temple into fragments of pebbles, leaving behind only the pestilence of death. In accordance with the annals of the written Scriptures, a body of writings regarded as authoritative according to historical data, the total eradicated by Samson by far surpassed the quantity he destroyed while Judge of Israel. All narratives upon this topic, relying heavily on much authenticity of the description itself, nevertheless relate the perfect manifestation of faith and, if conscientiously affected by the veneration of the topic itself, the conviction of truth, I hope will invade the permanent stream of consciousness of the multitude.

Since the dawn of history, marked by the innumerable illustrations, faithful people have been well compensated in their foregone conclusion. But during the customary duration of life, as fashioned in the destiny of Samson, not even the strongest will escape the uttermost agonies that will emerge within the scope of human existence. The Book of Job, an extended narration rendering further testimony of faith, illustrates a man of comfortable means, characterized with a generously lavish amount of wealth. The infinite miseries that overwhelmed the quiescent spirit of Job grew inconceivably hideous, compelling him to experience the evils of a horrible nightmare, making it impossible to awake from the depths of a slumberous agony. Job is afflicted with a grave disease, a state of decay that consumes his body. As the misfortunes grasped him fiercely by surprise, shaking the very base of his soul, Job's wealth reversed so he found himself with the economic status of pauperism. The duration of the catastrophe inclusively prevailed upon Job's children, extending the immediate effects of death to them. God, through his omnipotent wisdom in disclosing a divine truth without supernatural means and by removing his designed shield of protection over Job, had permitted Satan to premeditate crimes of evil against Job, distinctly and unquestionably exposing to view the faithful attributes in Job. In a single devastating blow the disarrangement of Job's life was initiated by a rushing annihilation, ghastly permeating his whole being with demonic passion of sorrow. Struggling in vain to decrease the anxiety that arrived, Job requested to presence of the glorious strength of his soul to combat the sweeping images of suffering that prevailed. With his once definite soul against the indefinite wretchedness, Job most vividly desired death, cursing the day of his birth. He endeavored to summon courage, prompting the necessity to seek an answer for the consequence of his affliction. As Job approached God with his dilemma, self-assured with eagerness, and with the anticipation of a merciful relief, Job's question was considered, but he was pacified with the answer that God is the Omniscient. Faith kept Job from the precipice. Job's preeminent faith predisposed God to reward him with an abundant supply of love and the delight of affluence. The essence of this literature, the product of an extensive interpretation, has inspired me to maintain my faith, touching me to the heart—expecially when such facts originate from a source so avowedly and proverbially virtuous, the Bible. My critical thoughts are considerably centered, expressing an opinion of much delicacy on this topic, in the belief that the trials and tribulations that encompass our lives are tests of faith.

I shall endeavor to express directly, pungently, and altogether more to the purpose the historical events of countless people who, having sufficiently endured the test of faith, as I share with you the following related stories as passing thoughts, were recipients of the gracious approbation of God for their admirable steadfastness. In the Old Testament, the literary genesis of mankind, Noah was instructed, fully touched with God's magnanimous sacredness, with the miraculous task of building an ark, an outlet with the single proceeding of saving his family and different species of animals. Noah's character was possessed of the natural effect of faith, for God found Noah to be consistent with standards of what was fair, upright, and moral. Noah, maintaining a firm conviction in God and acting upon the spirit of this principle, faithfully accepted God's command, which, in its natural condition, met with an occurrence of success. Abraham's faith was placed upon the brink when he was to offer his son as a sacrifice. The mode of disposing of his son was designed by God to examine the amount of devotion in Abraham. When the evidence was confirmed, a voice emerged from the Heavens, stopping abruptly the sacrificial demonstration, giving credibility to Abraham's steadfast adherence to the principle of faith. The recognition of additional identities that augment the particulars of my narration echoes through the history of mankind. Abel and Cain, Moses, and Christ are men that positively warrant my conclusion. Each one is multiple evidence, built upon multiple proof. The most vigorous of human investigation will attest to my findings. In the midst of the emotional interaction, the probability of doubt merely falls into accumulative skepticism.

You have already fathomed the fullest intimacy of my mind, educed from my written words chiefly to show you the spirit of my soul that came forth. I forever will bear in memory the lasting examples of the many faithful people mentioned, and of the unmentioned, who because of their iron love for God inherited everlasting qualities with an unceasing radiation of happiness. My mental collectedness, the result of intense research to which I have alluded previously, was more forcibly impressed with the elaborate splendor of faith. If I have failed in any attempt to convey the full concept of the precise character of my literature or of the history therof, I will hold in my heart an amplification of pain for the wastefulness of my endeavors. My writing on faith, incorporating the wisest and safest method possible, was based upon the principle of human action, using my thoughts on what I did, rather than upon the basis of what the Almighty intended me to do. As I grow wiser as a result of my experience, the unconquerable force of my total comprehension, sustained by the inclination of my thoughts, has convinced me that in the abyss of time lies my unlimited test of faith. If in my religious endeavors I still cannot understand the visible work of God, how then in his invisible thoughts? The sublime theme of my prayers continues to strengthen my faith, as I labor incessantly to prove myself worthy of the boundless generosity of God.

IV
Inculpable Sin: A Bitter Taste of Death

What prudence invaded the perimeter of my fundamental logic when I, resolving the necessity of a persistent issue, focused on the title *Inculpable Sin: A Bitter Taste of Death.* Amid the ubiquity of death, engulfing the mixture of my physical and mental qualities, the title meandered inadvertently through the channels of my thoughts, permanently heading the course of action of my literary endeavors. Nothing could surpass the reverent opportunity to indulge in comments about the temporary insanity that afflicted my son, eternally tainting our constitutions with the extreme fury of grief, pain, and sorrow. Each extreme induces the others, with the unfortunate occasion when the multitude of extremes is the affair of a moment. It is a sad truth that is conveyed through the profound reflections of a father's mystification consuming the heart, enervating the soul, and absolutely destroying the enthusiasm of life. The many unanswerable questions that propounded my mind strengthen my self-imposed sense of obligation, striking me with morally bound thoughts for the benefit of others.

Catholicism, a religious branch of knowledge, imbued with the fundamental principles of life, as well as most general causes of the universe, professes that suicide, setting forth explicitly the statement with the essential meaning and characteristics of the word, is the voluntary termination of one's life while in full possession of one's faculties. Notwithstanding and in defiance of its own doctrine, the church is advancing gradually, coping with the increasing dilemma, questioning not only the act of the individual, but whether that individual was really in full possession of his faculties. While the church dwelt upon its peculiarities of insensitivity, unanimously centered in disregard of the construction of causes and effects, it would deprive these unfortunate souls of ecclesiastical burial, inappropriately piling the consistency of lack of logic in thought upon the wretched act. In the execution of any punitive retribution, nothing that the learned call justice will make two wrongs make one right. At this precise moment in time, as I cursively pen the present circumstance, temporary insanity is presumed, allowing a Christian burial as a gesture of understanding rather than a gesture of condemnation. As I inquire further into the vitally important belief of the church, it is still the indubitable fashion of Christian law to consider suicide a mortal sin that infringes on God's will, jeopardizing divine mercy to one's immortal soul. Only the Almighty, Lord of life and death with infinite power, may consent to suicide. I discovered at length through the detailed analysis of the Bible incredible references concerning saints who killed themselves out of a desire for martyrdom or to preserve chastity. The accounts of these suicides, to my excessive astonishment, relating the exploits of a discriminating interest that suddenly overpowered my emotions, are satisfactorily interpreted as divine inspiration by which God allowed the action or by the singular circumstance of "inculpable ignorance."

According to Judges, Samson's self-destruction, the former illustration embodied in my composition, as I call upon you in supplication to take into due consideration, is not classified as suicide but an indirect kiling of himself. He was permitted to die because of his fallibility. This avenue of death, permitted to function under certain conditions, is noted as the Principle of Double Effect. This is a concept designed to determine whether or not a specific act that manifests itself with two effects, one good and one bad, is a sin. The following conditions must be present to make such an act lawful: the act itself must not be a sin, the bad effect must not be intended but only permitted, the good effect must not follow from the bad effect, and there must be a good enough reason for permitting the effect.

I am to the fullest extent cognizant, also powerless to unearth this truthful thought from my heart, that there can be no logical explanation in our era of human existence, especially with our general whims of human action, or no justifiable rhetoric that will suffice for permitting such an effect as suicide. With the evidence against my beloved unfolded, characterized by the omission of that which is positive, I find it extremely painful when the populace surround themselves with the credence that my son committed a mortal sin. With the excessive pain that envelopes me, confirming the declaration with a thousand affirmations, I am possessed with the inability to arrest the power of their understanding to inculcate the documentary evidence of my thoughts, totally disturbing the state of my equilibrium. It is unrealistic to contradict the emission of excellent reasons and to stifle thoughts that hinge from the most pious convictions. With a heavily convulsive disorder that completely electrifies my nervous system, and in spite of any efforts to prevent the execution of such electric current, I strive with an insatiable appetite to assuage the inquietude of my heart. I have presumed, basing my hypothetical presumption on the pure analogy of thought, eliciting mental endeavors from the boundlessness of love for my son, that his inconceivable deed, seemingly contradictory like the many facets of a problem, be cataloged as an inculpable sin, equalizing the actions of saints that succumbed in inculpable ignorance. The bulk of thoughts that I have penned is a paradox.

It is well within the residency of my thoughts and emotions that God will mercifully manifest partial forgiveness on my son. He who was unrighteous was ignorant of God's will. Had he been touched with the keenest perception of so wonderful a manifestation of God's will, the unrighteousness of instant destruction would have never traversed the fortress of his thoughts. The commanding impetuosity that extinguished his life absolutely absolved him from his inculpable sin. His unbearable weight of anxiety could not be overcome, rendering him an object for total ruin under the circumstances. Let it not be inferred, by any stretch of the imagination, from what I have just written that I have detailed a mere fancy or penned a narrative of mysticism.

As I proceed on the same avenue to detail my undisputable logic, the most important and relevant of all the truths about the title of my book, I cannot reject a matter of great consequence that lay in the composure of my son's personality. From the initial phase of his infancy, naturally temperamental, my son was noted for his elaborate disposition and consumed frame of mind. Reminiscing upon the memories of his tender youth, during the delicate period of his mental cultivation, I recall certain prevailing events that unequivocally startled and utterly awed us. My wife, immeasurably alarmed with his unbearable burden, significantly recorded the course of his comportment to the fragile age of six months.

I am well apprised with God's apperceptive plan to allow his creation the undeniable opportunity to develop wisdom and character by free choice. I do perceive the reason to question, therefore, whether a tender and undeveloped mind really possesses the intelligence to comprehend his own actions. Indeed, I am inclined to believe, for it is evident, that certain behavior is innate, considering respectively the qualities that were deeply rooted and firmly ingrained in my son's character. He was overwhelmed by his predestined malady. As Albert grew older, he was unanimously consumed by an unpredictable drive, an unnatural excess of pain inflicted during his brief tenure of life. There is a great perception on my behalf, especially under the present circumstance, amidst my agony and the simple powers of my mind, about Satan's efforts to completely ruin human beings, destroy all cultures, pervert attitudes, and inject emotions that eventually bring total destruction. He implants evil attitudes, an ineluctable force, in young minds to induce them to believe that this is the way of life. We as parents, in an absolute state of constant intense emotion, must endure the struggle against this inextricable dilemma.

And at length, of all the infallible solutions that ruffle the composure of my mind without negating the truth, and that irritate me beyond endurance, the majority of the responsibility emphatically rests upon my shoulders. With a painful confession I submit to the intolerable guilt that persecutes the corners of my mind and the chambers of my heart. I was ignorant of the fact, classifying my frustrated explanation as poor justification, that he was overwhelmed by anxiety and constantly facing the reality of death. The hereditary temper of my son that tormented his life, seizing him violently beyond comprehension, caused him to be in dire need of my understanding and a greater symmetry of love. Because of the improper proportion of his harmony, the unwholesome condition of his character, I unconditionally exculpate him from the inscrutable act that afflicted his soul. As the scrutiny of my senses detected a crevice in his spirit, for it was not totally probable that the actuality could have escaped conspicuous observation, I did not perceive the warning of the tempest, a tempest that swept us in the vortex of doom. As I reminisce on the memory of the horror, extending far down into the residence of my soul, I cannot divorce myself from guilt, the culpability of failing to enlighten him with the spiritual knowledge to resolve his emotional problems in life. My inquisitiveness never entertained the suspicion. My mental acquisitiveness did not grasp the clue to institute an organized search for the summary of his actions. Confidently depending on the positiveness of nature to absolve the ill-favored effect of the abnormality, I busied myself in the collection of my ignorance. At length I have arrived at the extent of my comprehension, a conclusion containing a summary of what preceded, which, a profitable experience for the populace if so desired, wrought in me no wonder in resolving the truth. Why I had not arrived at it before is obvious. I discovered what I sought, the fault. I confess, condemning myself with shame, to being guilty as charged. I made up my mind that it is more sinful, positively ugly, and extremely unrefined to find fault with the conduct of my son's inculpable sin.

V
Why Pain and Death?

In the course of each day, as I leisurely peruse the newspaper, in quest for no immediate issue, I acquire inadvertently a mental exasperation, indeed, to my utter amazement, from the voluminous publication of human deaths in the world, which in proportion has become a measure of great vexation observed in the history of human misery. These incensed revelations of the horrid affairs of babies dying at birth, of the accounts of old people dying in their sleep, and of the rampant growth of adolescents dying tragically and, without a doubt, while disturbing the serenity of some people have motivated within the real character of my personage, as it is impossible to conceive my amazement, numerous inquisitions pertaining to pain and death. God's insensibility, standing at an extended distance aloof from the miseries of life, enduring through the faculties of the soul and what seems to be a lack of comprehension of the true state of affairs with his creation, continues to exist perenially as the ultimate subject of discussion. It did occur to me, therefore, rendering an uncontrollable desire, that it might be well to initiate an investigation why God ignores the cries of the desolate and thence research the immense mystery that baffles the multitude. The gloomy memory of my son's death, too consequential a nature in the phenomenal contemplation of life, prompted me, amid the encompassing air of sheer madness, a frenzy that also enveloped the great aptitude of my thoughts, to reckon with the whole thrust of the matter in question. My insatiable craving for knowledge, a mental expedition undertaken with deliberate consideration, channeled my judicious quest to the depths of the Bible. There, thoroughly absorbed in the determining process of critical examination, of what may be termed analytical investigation or classified as philosophical reasoning from a perception of the interrelations of the sacred book, the literary merits, theologically indited to prescribe modes of moralistic or respectable relationships intrinsic to life, conclusively endorse the genesis of guilt to Adam and Eve. By a singular circumstance, relating to their devilish exploits of eating the forbidden fruit, they ignominiously acquainted the natural descent of people with sin, the willful violation of divine law—pain, the unpleasant physical sensation resulting from injury, illness, or other physical disorder; and death, the adequate consequence for all mankind for the intensity of their sin of disobedience. This deliberate inception of voluntary disobedience, an evil feeling that took possession of their senses, constituted the opportunity of transmitting to mankind the process of making decisions of "good and bad" and "right and wrong." For that moment of intense horror some unaccountable terror crept by degrees into their spirit, instantaneously overwhelming future generations with he inevitable avenue of death. The credulous Eve, designed with a deficiency of imagination, was unable to detect the falsity of the tempting Satan; the susceptible Adam, afforded with an aridity of genius, could not provide eloquent imagination from his rigid thought to expose as false the tempting words of the credulous Eve. Upon the whole, losing the grace of God, both were rendered notorious, unfavorably ostracized from the garden of perfection. The difficulties encountered in regard to their disobedience set the precedent for similar future actions, compelling mankind to choose between these rigorous choices of good and bad. The principal loss was the guarantee of eternal life. It succumbed, forcing the conception of our own destiny. Irrespective of the consequences, without regard to themselves or consideration for God's command, they proceeded.

As I hover between memories and my irresolute state, the hues of my life are a result of the struggle in my endeavors to overcome the undesirable dilemma of right or wrong thrust upon the world by Adam and Eve. Upon a considerable amount of energy, invested in my inquisition, my labor has extracted the veracious conclusion that thenceforward we have been mainly influenced by the vices of the world that are deeply entombed in our own hearts, undeniably descending from our original ancestors. The vicissitudes of human affairs will most definitely unleash effects of thoughtlessness on the greatest part of our lives. We may assume to vindicate ourselves by seeking the power of God in our souls, but the ultimate vindication will come when we succumb for our sins. It is absolute chaos, far beyond the realm of conceivability, proceeding judiciously with commendable prudence, to live gracefully without God in our hearts. Even in the extremeness of a perfectly impeccable manner, bethinking a life-style with soundly good intentions, can we unanimously exercise sound judgment in the course of each day.

There is a precise correlation, a facsimile in human comportment, between my son's choice of temptation and that of Adam and Eve. The exact duplication of their fate, influenced through the evil dominance of Satan, was the convulsive choice of death. When we reflect how very common we find it in our power to make decisions, since it has repeatedly happened thenceforth, we must truthfully admit, without hesitation, that we do not perceive with full cognizance the critical nature of each decision.

In the summation of my narrative, including the profound topic of choice within us, pain and death are attributed to the tree of knowledge of good and bad. In the former, the unendurable oppression is perpetual; in the latter, consuming. There is nothing more agonizing than the ultimate fate of dying. The prescription and peculiarity of our deaths, arranged to unfold in various avenues, are easily effected by God, so that every event is well adapted with extreme precision upon our lives at the least expected moment. Fearful indeed is the doom. But if we creduously acknowledge God through faith, then we must willfully accept the suffering of pain and death. It is inconceivable, even of those with an avid observation of human nature, to prevent an act of God. Death, the inseparable companion of mankind, is the human epilogue of life. Every species of profound misery will befall upon our human vitality, enveloping us within the bounds of God's understanding to caress our hearts with comfort while in the midst of our dreary solitude.

VI
What Is Death?

What is death? The universe is indeed cognizant of multitude endeavors by men of extreme genius who have enlightened us with their condescending thoughts about death. This demonstrable existence, exalted opinions that have greatly dignified the inevitable mystery of life, has become so generously approbated by numerous magnificent scholars of our era. In spite of the attraction of universal contribution, the extremity of their differences, vanquishing the constraint of my fears, has conscientiously obliged me to sufficiently pen my known convictions of death. To elevate myself to a feeling of self-condemnation, I therefore contend, gracefully admitting sufficient intensity to express my self-dictating masterpiece of eloquence, that my thoughts, contributed by the hardship of experience, is altogether more to the purpose and, without a doubt, more direct.

Since the time of evolution, partaking in thoughts that have stirred the essence of my mental faculties, mankind has demonstrated an infinite concern with the morbid extravaganza of death. The multitude of instances has rendered evidence that it does not discriminate. For the longest time I was overpowered by the greatest involuntary sense of confusion, arousing in me a sickening fury that pervaded my mental efforts with the eagerness to die. A conglomerate of individuals in the world, sharing a saturated catalog with different conjectures respecting death, have shown an affection far more passionate than common.

The speculation on death has utterly demonstrated in many an anxiety of fear, resigning themselves to the peculiar state of helplessness. Others, obstinately persistent in their thoughts, have given evidence of apprehension, producing an overpowering sense of health implications within themselves. At length, having come to the insoluble problem, the conspicuous nature of their resistance is simply the suffocating fear of dying. Few, or in the sparse population of any, at least, are in full possession of their senses.

The incipient pursuit of knowledge, relying to a small extent on the mere minimal usage of *Webster's Dictionary*, led me to consider one definition of death as "the end of life: the act, process, or fact of dying." Guiding the essence of my research to the Book, the Bible, which depicts in words a deep and reverent awe, reveals that death is for man the termination of mortal life, causing the cessation of spiritual life. There can be no doubt of the genuine truth, as I give a verbatim translation, that man's soul is preliminarily designed to return to its Maker, who with a magnanimous gesture of clemency will appropriately transform the body to dust of the Earth. Since the garden of Eden, the body of man is said to be by nature mortal. Death, the expiration of time on Earth, is for mankind.

At no time in history, as I retrospectively survey the daily curriculum of this country, have people, involving an affirmative degree to some extent, appealed more to the thought of self-preservation than they do at this present juncture. This passionate fervor, excessively pleasant, making the sacrifice worthy of reward or praise, has been woven together to form ardent attitudes that can be detected particularly through the special diets for its effects on the body and by the intricacies of their exercising adventures. My literature may sound didactic, overly inclined to moralize, but that is not the fundamental ingredient of my story that I endeavor to project. The intensity of gratification sought in longevity has been the disenchantment of our society. The delirium en bloc, so great in possession of blindness, so great in exhibition of simplicity, and so great in extension of shallowness, happening to fall upon the sole fancy of their habitual repetition of actions, has become most definitely the essence of their existence. People relish zestfully the application of renascence, rejecting the most obvious process in the world as old age. Most people patronize the duration of youth, wincing at the thought of death. Upon the whole, our society has developed from a variety of people with a sort of inconsistent modes of thought.

We commemorate the origins of a life with the passion of jubilee, harmoniously inspiring us with a nostalgic sentiment of great magnitude. As that life gradually advances extensive moments at the expense of birthdays, accompanied by the intensity of full knowledge from others, a feast to solemnize that birth is in order. I know the contrary to be the case in the sensations of death. This occasions me little, if any, amazement. The principal thought that pervades my mind, with the keenest curiosity about the expectation, is the paltry consideration devoted in honor of the dead. Some uncannily negate, at various instances, the full, intricate process of the chronological order of events, that being birth, life, and death. I am cognizant of the fact, as the ultimate thing becomes more and more evident, that only inanimate objects live forever. It has not been firmly impressed upon the powers of our mind, a mentality sparsely capacitated with the interest of dying, to prepare ourselves for the particular horror of death. Among the hereditary attributes we possess, none is more solid than the denying attitude concerning dying. After due deliberation, I have firmly resolved that even though life is proceeded upon with an all absorbed interest, enhanced through the increasing vitality of self-preservation, death will occur with incredible swiftness to the multitude regardless of any sustained efforts to survive. Upon this we must endeavor an effort to cultivate our minds, elucidating ourselves with the reality of death, the indispensable appointment of destiny.

During the course of history, mankind has undoubtedly experienced death in infinite varieties. In ancient, diverse cultures, having grasped and assimilated facts to my satisfaction, death was a transition from the status of life into another status actuating after death. Without much desperation, an affirmed few have obliged themselves sagaciously with a belief in the genuine powers of reincarnation, a process of reinstating a soul again into execution in the world. Confined in this particular stage of life, invariably engraved in the immediate intelligence of so many credulous individuals, not only is this delicate phenomenon a significant factor in their lives, but it unfolds a crucial and an integral part in their attitudes toward death. Concluding with a mere fact, as I rely heavily upon the vast benefit of my literary research, I am compelled to vociferate that death is not a final state if one possesses a firm conviction of life after death. This sentiment, methodically induced through the teachings of the church, which is a medium that mellifluously reached large audiences, becomes beneficial so that one may perceive dying with a scrupulous thought. There is much consistency over the years, characterized by the same course of action taken by relatives, when it comes to the angusih that lingers in their hearts. In dying, rendering themselves unto dissolution, people are liberated instantaneously from the root of their most overwhelming problem, while their relatives drown with a mournful sensation that impregnates the depths of their souls, unleashing a deep feeling of mortal sorrow.

Some people shudder at the very thought of death, and they dread any species of horror that will venture forth from future events. In regard to the preceding statement, peculiarities in the mere fashion of deplorable follies, psychologists, expounding their theories in great detail, have observed that most people who are affected by the intolerable effects of fear of death at an early age will not struggle in extremity to overcome the incoherence of the trepidation in their later years. The association of fear is none, and the results of the absolute effect will influence the spirit of their existence and the feature of their mental condition. There is forever, till doomsday as a matter of fact, and understandably so, a sustained and qualified tendency of predicating the cardinal point of death in the church. But as human nature prevails in all of us, it is readily understood as true that, within an impenetrable fastness, we undervalue the significance of death, which then becomes irrelevant to us.

Expatiating upon the array of details that exquisitely bear upon moral dignity of patients who are anticipating death through terminal illnesses, doctors make reference to the internal anxiety that pours impetuously from those patients who, while lacking a mere sense of magnificence, resort to the natural tendency of anger. Patients, emotionally agitated by the ghastly and unexpected revelation, struggle within themselves in vain with all the anger that may be engendered, befitting in its immensity to the horror fallen upon their mortal soul. They become alienated from the world, consumed in the indulgence of the natural tendency of hate, with an opposing and antagonistic sentiment about death. Though the avenues of death lie in the extremity, none surpasses the immense quantity of bewilderment rendered from the violent impression of suicide.

Although low in spirits from the tormented conclusion of dying, a patient may overcome the palsying condition that took complete possession of his mind to finally realize peace with himself, his loved one, and God. But a patient with the tormented knowledge of dying or any condition of abnormality that leads to the intolerable actuality of death may fashion his or her thoughts to accomplish an everlasting peace with the whole world for that matter. The principal thought altogether is that the patient resolves within himself to compensate others for his wrongful and unsuitable deeds. The patient, having at length put the mind in a state of favorable civility, commences to endure the unwholesome truth, anticipating the moment when the final breath will flee the habitation of its existence. But the enigmatic mystification of suicide seizes relatives with a permanent incoherence of the mind, succeeding perfectly in deadening the sensitivity of their hearts. One's incertitude about the particulars in the matter will contribute to heighten the mystery of the suicidal circumstance. No matter what painful circumstance of death unfolds, no matter what freak accident evolves, and no matter what unaccountable gesture of fate envelops our lives, we must endeavor to actuate a semblance of strength for our own benefit; and as the calamitous cessation of humanity invades the privacy of our thoughts, a prayer will deliver us from under the auspices of imagination to the authenticity of reality.

And now, through the fullest tormented memoirs of my mental faculties, as I beckon to arrest the memory of my son, after having related all my harassing thoughts about death, I endeavor to recall the unmeasured consultation that was once vociferated by our priests. Spoken with distinct enunciation, favorably accepted and conclusive in every aspect, the superiority that senior priests affirmed, outweighing in assertion their younger and less experienced counterparts, was an effective oral communication that will resound eternally through the length of our existence. I remember well, with a sentiment of gratification, that day of bewilderment when I pondered the total consummation of my son's fate. It becomes extremely necessary to pay reverent regard to Father Mitchell, naturally passionate and caring in the midst of our frantic grief. His visitation, a day after the loss of our son, to a home that was typically sentimental with the emotions of love like in the environment of most dwellings, was a determined effort of heart on his behalf, to impart an understanding and the appropriate conversation that would eventually submit to that fateful day of intense distress and the pain of our hearts. His initial statement, penetrating to the depth of our being, produced a profound positiveness that emphasized the benevolence that ruled as the sovereign ingredient in our son's personality. Without ever actuating Albert's acquaintance, Father Mitchell assured us convincingly that the consuming thoughts of benignant people seldom develop into the rigorous anxiety of hurting others, just themselves. The total consciousness of his conversation, stated confidently by his most sacred oath, was that if our son had been morally inferior, he could have earnestly facilitated the death of his girl friend instead. We, with the consciousness that eternally accompanies the nature of our thinking hidden immeasurably deep in the shelter of our hearts, knew that our son, in spite of the perplexing nature of things, was an exceptional human being and was the ardency within our hearts that fell from the expanse of the heavens. Need I say more? Upon the whole, Albert was the sustenance of our lives that rendered us happy.

Even in the midst of an improbable dream, bowing

with a sense of acknowledgment, do I qualify within the perimeters of my education to stand in opposition to the foremost professions of our times, such as science, medicine, or philosophy, when their inspired assertions dubiously endeavor to determine the moral character of death? The analytical process, blessed with the necessary ingenuity of leading authorities in said fields, is one that is remarkably incapable of explanation. The ingenious observations of the experts, which envelop the realm of the imagination of mere mortals, do convey an immediate philosophy very strictly analogous. But the whole distinctness of their literature, being vacant in simple communication, is not ingenuous. Their concepts fall in the shadows of linguistic imagination, or as my narrative has purely injected, the character of their thoughts has succumbed within the vicinity of sheer fancy. I now come, occupied with burdensome thoughts, rendering myself to the wild fervor of insanity, to convey an abstract sentiment, a personal explication of death that I hope will occupy the mental emotions of the people with a simplicity they easily can afford. My own intimate knowledge of death, as I detail with candor the infinity of mental anguish, will not hesitate to confess laconically the ghastliest of pains that has dwelt in the seat of my emotions. Death is irrepressible. It is an emptiness in the heart that, with irresistible memories, fills a lifetime with the persistence of a sensory impression of a loved one that will linger beyond the test of time. Death, a monstrous natural phenomenon, manifesting itself in distinctive possibilities, is thrust upon us, leaving us in an excruciating and agonizing state of mind. Our sentient minds, the sentry box of our memories, will entertain fervent thoughts, while awake or asleep, of our loved ones that exist within ourselves alone. Only the memories that are buried in the deepest corners of our mind, buried in the fathomless chambers of our hearts, will procrastinate concerning the evanescence of death. The endeavor of my thoughts will inevitably unleash a dolorous sensation as I retrieve the lovely image of my son.

VII
Why Do People Commit Suicide?

As I pen a mystery of life, I cannot help but dwell on meditative thoughts, busying myself with the incontrovertible madness of suicide. It is my contention, expressing it with an unwonted emotion, that the countenance of these victims becomes so vigorously saturated by external problems that they apparently submit to the thought of failure. Their thoughts, pervading their every mental extremity with a sense of hopelessness, fall into incoherence, effectively denying them the solutions to their most pressing problems. A person, typically of a species without perseverance, one of the human race that invariably exists, not endowed with any semblance of courage to endure any state of severe affliction, will regard any kind of minimal or unsubstantial happening as an insolvable tribulation. A tender mind, particularly one not in full possession of its mental faculties, one not endowed with the inherent power of bearing up under hardships, may rebel in itself, thus destroying the body, the very essence of its existence. The acute vulnerability cannot overcome the thought of suicide as the process of ascertaining the state of insouciance, a condition of being free from worry. It is not unusual to contaminate our thoughts with suicidal tendencies when overwhelmed by discontented circumstances. Even personalities that possess a considerable amount of knowledge through their experiences may have contemplated the feeble thought. But to engage venturously in the capacity to fulfill the fatal transaction requires a profusion of hopelessness. Although suicide is never justified, the victims become mesmerized by the unwarranted act. They realize their unceasing pursuit, bewildering their relatives with the nature of their undue decision. The very thought of the decision dims our lives in proportion with each occasion when we fully turn our attention upon it.

Practically every day, merely in pursuance of my daily habit of reading the newspaper, my sense of sight is drawn sagaciously to the multiplicity of suicide reports. In spite of the newspaper being densely cluttered with the usual occurrences of this nature, each ignominious act differed as to cause. The quality of concern in suicides in this country is wavering by the very mode of investigations, lacking in the more refined ability for comprehension.

I was astonished profoundly, mentioning it unhesitatingly, by the momentous discovery that other countries had suicide as part of their culture. It was a distinct honor for people to give their lives for justifiable causes. The intensity of my research was not ordinary and was in the capacity of being too profound. Retracing the steps of history through the multitude of cultures, the annals of antiquity, having readily shown their valid credentials of ancient time collectively, show evidence that suicide was a designated way of ending one's life if one was bored with living and wanted to die. The following are the collections of selective testimonies respecting the distinctive values of suicide, commonly endeavored by the foremost countries of our times. I strive to pen these facts chiefly for the sake of strengthening my contention on the idea of self-destruction.

In Japan, one of the most eminent cultures that is utterly unequaled in the world, the distinguished people of high rank and the illustrious noble class, both classifications of people characterized with the qualities of excellence, practice seppuku (hara-kiri), a form of suicide by disembowelment. The nature of the wound upon their own person, an inevitable affection of noble quality, is provided for the elite if they have fallen into the confines of disgrace. The act, the most exorbitant demonstration of courage, is an acquittal for a dishonorable situation, restoring social status to the person and the family. During the attack on Pearl Harbor, on that Day of Infamy, the Japanese pilots were assigned to kamikaze planes to execute suicidal crashes on American ships. These pilots, embraced by a profound sense of suicidal deliverance, were honored by glorious funeral ceremonies before they left Japan, expecting to perish while executing their missions.

In China a bride carried a dagger as a permanent decoration of the wedding gown. The bride had no alternative but to commit suicide if the marriage failed. And when the occasion demanded it, the culture entirely observed nothing distinctive about the concept of self-destruction. Upon examining the chillness of the mode, I find no escape from the conclusion of misunderstanding the nature of the custom. It is only left for us to view this custom as confounded and appalling, with extreme horror and disbelief. Because of our state of mind, somewhat more particular in the endeavors of logic, the science of correct reasoning, it is our part to condemn the life-style, existing so unequivocally in this manner.

Let us now focus the full powers of our mental abilities on the American Indian, whose customs suggested effectively the equal evidence of disbelief. In some American tribes, traditionally characterized by their own suicidal customs that were imbedded since the genesis of time, it was designed by custom that the wives of the chief had to engender their own deaths when he died. Their self-destruction was to signify faithful devotion and to provide eternal companionship to the chief in the other world. The wives, being in great number, had sufficient reason to exhibit the greatest evidence of all the noble qualities of love. The first one who would accomplish her own death vigorously would unquestionably be the preferred wife for the chief in the other world. This was the ultimate compensation for a faithful wife who publicly displayed magnificent devotion, thus avoiding a dismal solitude for the chief. This is a belief absolutely alien to our present society, a foreign impression whose motives have existed in the extremity of antiquity. We dare not find this butchery in the fancy of our intelligence.

There have existed innumerable circumstances that, falling outside the bounds of the habitual establishment of custom, were employed to resolve the gravity or peculiar state of a situation. The value of the decision was much greater than the intolerable horror of suicide. Upon the occasion there was meaning. In A.D. 73, the Roman procurator of Judea, Flavius Silva, attacked the impregnable fortress of Masada with his formidable Tenth Legion of Roman soldiers. After a lapse of some months, spent fighting against all odds, the Jewish people, under the command of Elezar ben Ya'ir, deprived their enemy of complete victory by committing suicide. The decision, a matter that is considered within the bounds of human dignity to the Jewish nation, was prompted to avoid surrender, cruel punishment, and slavery at the hands of the Roman Empire. These Jewish zealots caused total astonishment to the enemy, performing not out of desperation but from pride and religious belief. If there is any consolation in the act of their decisive shudder, they did die in a state of freedom.

In the year 42 B.C., Marcus Junius Brutus, a Roman statesman persuaded to join the conspiracy against Julius Caesar, committed suicide to make restitution for his involvement in the assassination of the emperor. The act of suicide was completely contrary to his philosophical principles of life, but suicide was the only compromise that would eventually restore his honor among his friends and the respect of his enemies.

Adolf Hitler's Third Reich, an empire of butchery that was to last a thousand years, came to a conclusive end when he, his wife, and some of his officers and their families committed suicide without a shudder. As the impossiblity to resist the advancing troops absolutely unfolded, Hitler's gratification was to deny the enemy complete victory by self-destruction, thus avoiding retribution for his monstrous exploits of cruelty to the whole world.

As the development of time has elapsed, more and more people, from all walks of life, have become unresistingly engrossed with the thought of suicide. As I betook myself to a more intimate process of investigating suicidal affairs, I came into the possession of a considerable amount of information, as reported by a great number of psychologists in this country. The reflection of my investigation suggested, which I found indeed a mystery impossible to explain, the existence of sexual gratification in suicide. The revealing circumstance has indeed impressed me with a sense of peculiarity, a quality of strange features to be long remembered and gingerly preserved in the files of my memory.

There is a peculiar belief in this country, quite imperishable in reality, that completely dominates in the matters of suicide. Suicide is seen as a nefarious deed, with an absolute and exceedingly capricious attitude. Even in the most remote circumstances of terminally ill cases, there are no allowances for suicide. In a world where much political unrest overflows, there is a spirit of resistance toward death. I at length recognize the passionate desire for life, an eager vehemence of longing for immortality that struggles desperately in the world. An uncompromising passion of infinite supremacy is manifested in other parts of the world through their invigorating sense of survival, surpassing the irresistible temptation of suicide that excels in a country where the spirit of God is sovereign and the reign of reason is supreme.

Voluminous literature, purposely intended for publication to enlighten the masses, relates to specific causes for suicide. My ultimate plan is to produce mental exposure to the causes so that the multitude, so readily perceptible with the intended effect of wisdom, may foresee instantly any change that may intrude on the ordinary character of a loved one. We must accommodate ourselves with the thought that there is undoubtedly a cause for every effect and that there is an effect for every cause. Some of the causes for suicide are as follows: desperation, fear, hopelessness, guilt, depression, anger, impotency, loss of a job, lack of attention, lack of love, loss of a spouse, loss of a girl friend or boyfriend, loss of a parent, and a hundred other personal reasons a person may find. Sometimes when a person commits suicide, that person may even be trying to punish somebody else. After all the disappointments in life, the last setback becomes the offense that culminates in the final indignity of one's life, suicide.

Sigmund Freud, founder of modern psychiatry and psychoanalysis, believed that mental activity, an accurate understanding of a person's disposition, was the total domination that dictated the product of an individual's personality. He maintained through his observation of human behavior the stern influence that induced him to believe that the mind had three components, the id, the ego, and the superego. He communicated that the real characters of the three components would constantly be in conflict with each other. The conspicuous feature of the id was animalistic aggression and sexual gratification, possessing an unsatisfactory disposition of values, culture, and morals. The id, the unconscious that nurtured secret thoughts of absolute evil, was an inherited mental phenomenon from birth that denoted the infinite summary of negativism. From the suffocating environment of the id developed the ego, which helped neutralize the id by overpowering the primitive acts and forcing the id to stay within the framework of society and its rules. Freud asserted that from the ego developed the superego, where parental values, rules of conduct in society, cultural values, behavioral patterns, and guilt originated. When the id committed a lawless or disgraceful act, the superego would become guilty and worrried. The ego had not bothered to control the action, which indeed had resulted in negative consequences. Freud believed that when the id overpowered the other two components, then we had a maladjusted person (personality) in society. If all three components were in complete harmony with each other, then we had a well-adjusted person. All of the components developed interestingly enough, confronting each other intimately as the individual matured mentally.

Freud contended that when an individual committed suicide, the id (animal instinct) had dominated and overpowered the superego (parental values). The following observation confirmed by Freud has undoubtedly confounded and perplexed my mind into a pitiable state of ignorance, leaving me in an overwhelmed state of shock and total apprehension. Freud unfolds the startling statement that when an individual committed suicide, that individual was in reality not destroying himself but killing one of his parents. Freud indicated that the parental values had been overrun by the individual's personality of primitive instincts. When an individual was apparently confronted with the cause of a horrible occurrence, what lured him to suicide was not the immediate problem but the instant release of a deep-rooted hatred surfacing from the unconscious against one of the parents. This incomprehensible hatred had been excluded from the consciousness of the individual all along, existing only in the darkness of his unknown thoughts. I, with all the extreme exertion within me, have delved laboriously, with profound thoughts, into the deepest chambers of my heart and into the intellectual depths of my mind, to unanimously convince myself of confirming or repudiating the veracity of the previous theory. However, the nature of this theory is conceivable in some cases, but there is not sufficient evidence to warrant this belief in my case. I am steadfast in my conviction, possessing insurmountable faith, that it is absolutely impossible to imagine a parallel between the profound theory of Freud and the actuality of my son's death. I do possess, with a deep sense of understanding, the mentality to distinguish between the cause and effect of suicide in Freud's theory. Furthermore, the pure acquiescence of the reasoning and the conclusion involving my son's suicide has been diminished totally, the cause justifiably obliterated from my mental state, with only the absolute effects remaining.

Other noted psychologists have indicated that suicide is a confession to some extent. To the members of the laity, uncultivated minds, it is simply cowardice. It matters not, enduring the agitation that presents itself under this most unpleasant atmosphere, what the multitude vociferates. It is in pursuance of a fatherly love that I resolve unequivocally to collect my energies to defend my son's fallibility, even to the absolute extent of rage, if necessary.

Consider your conscience. Would it not be judged prudent to know your child preceding the horrible fact than to cry, "Why?" after the fact, engendering the tears before the grave?

VIII
Death Syndrome

Because of the composition at hand, the theme of death dominating the subject, I have come by profound research and observation to the conclusion that we possess a "death syndrome," a self-inflicting, prevailing tendency actuated readily through our every action in life. This syndrome is a fatalistic attitude that forces us to act out violent tendencies, self-destructive acts, self-punishing deeds, and reckless behavior. According to Sigmund Freud, we deliberately induce a "death instinct" that invariably drives us to our death, accelerating it with great deliberate speed, much faster than anticipated because we want desperately to return to where we originated. This reversion would be to a state of unawareness, as lifeless and inorganic matter. Because some people evidently produce, exhibiting with the greatest velocity, a much stronger desire to die, they are in constant conflict with the desire of self-preservation. People, overwhelmed by the desire of committing suicide, remove their lives out of existence, accepting wholeheartedly the evil of their situation, and willingly accept the responsibility of destruction at their own hand. While others, afraid of taking the full responsiblity at once, choose to die gradually by deliberately committing self-destructive acts, such as drinking, speeding, smoking, abusing drugs, and often fulfilling their professions. What produces an intensity of astonishment is the fact that some people committing these self-destructive acts in the presence of others, not only are these people inflicting punishment on themselves and others, but they are begging inadvertently for help. The utterance of ordinary speech, the expression of any subsequent conversation under certain circumstances, or the display of any action expresses the inner self of a person and, on occasions, reveals a deep-rooted problem suppressed in the mind since childhood. These acts, along with the death syndrome, facilitate misery and eventually their wish, death.

I now undertake the pursuit to convey a moderate account of the acts and professions aforementioned, particularly those that divert the fancy of many. Alcoholism, a social problem increasingly steadily beyond proportion each day, has never been classified or identified as a disease, only as a vice, a moral fault that produces, contrary to the mores, an undesirable behavior in society. Alcoholics, with an existing notoriety assumed by many decent people, engage in the consumption of liquor because of their inability to accept and cope with reality. They, intolerant of life's problems, attempt to drown their troubles, anticipating those troubles will vanish instantaneously the following day. People are encouraged to consumption by a full disclosure of valid reasons, credible excuses, and admirable motives. They become absorbed by a self-destructive path, possessing a fragile nature in their constitution. Taking into consideration the gravity of the situation, in pure confidence in my capacity, I have fully established an apparent conclusion, reflecting the obvious without much difficulty, that alcoholics stand in much need of attention, counseling, and the greatest of all cures, love.

The Bible speaks of the allowance of man to consume wine and other alcoholic beverages, for the fruits, grain, and honey were created to be man's enjoyment. The vice of excessive drinking has been considered a sin. The Holy

Scripture condemns overindulgence, a state of condition that constantly induces the evil that pervades the soul. Drunkenness, becoming a mortal sin when people lose their reason, weakens the character, ruins the health, impairs the personality, and destroys the mind. It brings about quarrels, anger, verbosity, and impurity. The church, leaving an atmostphere of enjoyment for its constituents, comparatively speaking, has never really condemned drinking completely. In order to cure the vice of drunkenness, not beyond the confines of achievement, and to some it's easier said than done, one must practice the virtue of sobriety. If not, God's anger will prevail and the happiness of Heaven will never be attained.

Driving, an easily accessible event that activates a diffusion in the death syndrome, effectually expresses much terror, particularly when speaking mostly of young people. I have occasionally made the acquaintance, reflecting an unnatural temperament on my part, of decent young people who transform themselves into monsters (with Dr. Jekyll and Mr. Hyde personalities) behind the wheel of an automobile, educing an unaccountable capacity for peril and death. I concur with a deep sentiment that the automobile is not the culprit, but the individual who seizes the opportunity to release a hidden violent disposition. Upon the multitude of reasons to consider in the unrelenting violence in young drivers, examining the facts cautiously, pressure appears as a predominant cause for luring such destructive effect. Young individuals, barricading themselves with an overwhelming stress, challenge death every day inadvertently behind the wheel of an automobile. It is my veracious contention, proceeding in the direction of decimating the immense pressure thrust upon our young people, that to combat this problem, one must exhibit love and reassurance in our every action toward them.

Smoking elicits an aggressive death syndrome, unleashing nicotine, a very poisonous oily liquid with a burning taste, occurring in tobacco. Addicted people continue to harass themselves in spite of the information about cancer linked to smoking. They derive pleasure from the agonizing mornings, incapable of breathing, bringing much stench of tobacco and stained teeth. They have become habitually shackled in the chains of cigarettes, contriving endless reasons not to abdicate the repulsive addiction of smoking, contumaciously accomplishing their self-destructive path. At any length it becomes evident, calling to mind the statistics on cancer linked to smoking, that many will lack willpower in their endeavors to quit, dying prematurely because of ignorance.

Drugs and other agonies atop the self-destructive path, consumed vigorously in wonted manner to alleviate pain or to reach a high mental state of delusion, hallucinating feelings that have no real cause, have infiltrated the criminal market in a short period. Drugs are gulped unhesitatingly by teenagers, and adults, for that matter, altering their lives, mentally and physically, leaving them in a reigning state of anomaly. A consuming curiosity pervades their mind about drugs, absorbing them with a shuddering insensitivity, luring themselves to a voluntary death. In the midst of the frenzied consumption of drugs, they unequivocally abdicate a sense of reality, never confronting their most demanding problems. Drugs become the whole essence of their lives.

I have previously signified professions exhibiting thrilling and perilous peculiarities, often enhancing the self-destructive path of the individuals. The most vivid and hideous jobs that are productive in extracting death wishes, making their influence excessively irresistible to most recipients, are auto racing, police work, flying, circus performing, coal mining, gambling, fighting fires, boxing, football, and daredevil exploits. These occupations, tantalizations adding a spice to life, have been refined and perfected, allowing the individual a much greater challenge in executing them.

In auto racing, where arenas with paved roads have been erected, sophisticated machines constructed, fireproof uniforms manufactured, and, most important, prize monies misappropriated, the performances have been accelerated to exploit the ultimate self-destructive desire in each racer.

Police officers, administrators of police work, dressed adequately with their uniforms and firearms, keep a twenty-four-hour vigil against the atrocities of human violence, defying death. They justify their death wish obstinately, indulging their appetite, disregarding their own lives for the safety of the public. This has been confirmed undoubtedly, noting with a distinctive affection of respectability that it requires a distinguished breed of people to assume the responsibilities of police work. Be that as it may, the profession provokes their death wish, unraveling new challenges each day.

Flying, the sky being the cemetery for pilots, unmistakably emits avariciously an exposition of death. Pilots, with an unparalleled excitement in the nature of flying, speculate unconsciously on the folly of the consequences of an undesirable accident, developing an incentive to challenge death.

The circus, where exploits of catastrophic performances present themselves, incessantly satisfies the actors' insatiable greed for death. Every act, a manifestation to show strength and skill, arouses a burning thirst that irresistibly consumes them in tantalizing death.

Coal mining, a vocation incurring extraordinary dangers and a high rate of fatalities and permanent injuries, exceedingly affects the workers with a lung disease known as neumonoultramicroscopicsilicovolcanoconiosis. The name, expressing an indication of astonishment and profound interest to many, is somewhat short in comparison to the multitude of lives it has devitalized. Even though miners assume the tremulous responsiblity of perfecting their field, they are cognizant of the perils implicated inclusively, becoming apprehensive in administering their jobs.

Gambling, forming the inevitable conclusion from its effects on people, has gradually approached the general consensus of being classified as a disease rather than a profession. Contrary to the multifarious opinions, gamblers anticipate wholeheartedly the affliction of losing rather than the thrill of winning, a dilemma displaying itself from the deep consciousness of the individual. Gamblers, unwilling to withdraw from the environment of self-destruction, unable to perceive a sense of danger to themselves, tragically begin to relinquish the possession of their soul. They proceed unceasing, defying the immense inequalities of losing, to savor the mysterious qualities inherited through gambling. In reality, every game becomes a sport of death.

Fire fighting, if properly observed, presents the most effectual peculiarity of pyromania, fascinating fire fighters with a distinctive obsession for death with fire. In the predicament of administering their job, confronting the natural sequence of an incineration, fire fighters tantalize death with a predominant adoration, extending from their suicidal patterns.

Boxing, a perpetually brutal sport, renders a violent physical struggle, discharging an undeniable death syndrome, leaving fighters in a precarious state of health. In defiance of the contemptuous and horrid carnage, boxers continue to satisfy their insatiable appetite for death. The deplorable passion of mankind to induce pain to each other, actuating itself through their own death design, has become an excessively complex problem in our society.

Football, America's most sophisticated sport, is so competitive that ruggedness is the authentic measure of a man. The occupants of the game, well trained and precisely fitted for their positions, undeniably entertain themselves in an atmosphere of death, discharging their most profound death syndrome, camouflaged in the profession of football.

Daredevils, a species of action-filled exhibitionists, infatuate themselves with the most incongruous deeds having a common characteristic of death. Each performance is tantamount to a confession of death.

These particular professions, to mention a few, extract the most fatalistic attitudes from each individual, unshackling a force of death in our society. There exists, observing in a very definite colossal proportion, other impressions of death syndromes, excessively appearing as slip-of-the-tongue mistakes or unconscious humor. The individuality of each personage languishes under the adoption of a less self-destructive scheme, insidiously making the pain less violent. Each individual dramatically illustrates a distinctive dimension of his own death syndrome, depending exclusively on the unparalleled state or condition of his mental endowments. We must undoubtedly resist the temptation of death, commanding our own disposition of life, by evaluating the acquisition of pertinent observations and data of ourselves through professional counseling.

IX
Socialization of Values

Socialization of values is the commanding process where a child will most definitely mold a unique personality, acquiring said distinction at the delicate stage of infancy. The development of a personality, therefore, reaching its climax at different ages and at various stages, possesses distinctive feelings, concepts, and behavior, interpreted and evaluated merely through the individual's own exploits. Values, ascertained from generation to generation, are the rules that permit or restrict the comportment of an individual in our society, relying heavily on the following five mainstreams of life: family, church, school, television, and friends.

The family is the primary institution that lays the basic foundation of the child's character traits, personal values, and personality. Parents have the sole responsibility of creating a proper environment, building the basic elements of understanding, discipline, guidance, independence, and, above all, love. A sincere love is conducive to harmonious life. Through my struggle in this turbulent world, I have come to confirm, cogitating with all the mediocre powers of my mind, that the essence of life is the ultimate gratification to be loved. I maintain that if a family is undermined by the consequences of the inability of weak parents, the child's character will not evolve to a normal degree of stability. The avenue to the achievement of a well-balanced personality is based on constant healthy examples from birth and the immeasurable exercise of love, a remedy prescribed by various psychologists. As another point of importance, parents should be cognizant of the tremendous advantage they possess. Children are credulous, believing everything parents say. The child's growth of the personality is vulnerable at this particular stage, necessitating a proper model to develop decisively. Initially, the parents determine and institute the spirit of the home, a natural and very justifiable obligation and a most judicious procedure that could be pursued incessantly. On infinite occasions, expressing my sentiments from statistics on families behaving without commendable moderation, children receive little or no encouragement from parents. An indeterminate aggregation of criticism consumes many parents, becoming highly critical of their children's every action. There is a decay of negative attitudes surrounding the family, discouraging its members with effective potency.

Our baffling economy, compelling parents compulsively out of their household into the labor force, an occurrence becoming so common, has vigorously destroyed the very basic unity of the family. The lack of supervision of children has absolutely stricken the family institution, the school system, and society, producing an incredible amount of disrespect, an exceeding magnitude of crime, but most of all, a perpetual destruction of our morality. Basic attitudes should originate from the family environment, setting forth a healthy view of life, and a social responsibility of involvement. A child begins to exercise, positively or negatively, the direct influences that parents transmit, directly or indirectly, establishing a path of success or a path of failure. My mental intuition on parental culpability, assiduously deducted through the annals of society, is that it is the ignorant blunder of not listening to our children. Children, because of their limited capacity, not enriched with the mastery of our vernacular language and not yet endowed with an extensive experience of life, attempt to communicate in their own respective words and behavior what they consider to be their most demanding and cumbersome problems. We permit inadvertently our difficulties to surround our mental propensities, ignoring the personal well-being of our children. Lack of attention is a particular deficiency in parents, sending distressing signals to young children that are easily discerned. If the appropriate guidance is absent, a child will absolutely become a malcontent, finding dreadful difficulty functioning sagaciously in society. We must cultivate our children to accept the challenges of society, confront the trials and tribulations of life, and learn with assiduity the teaching of Christ. Not only must we lay the foundation of encouragement and praise, but also the acceptance of the valuable learning experience of failure. I am convinced, contemplating this with reasonable reassurance, that there must be considerable room for failure in a child's life. Some parents insist on creating perfect children, placing strict and rigid demands on them. And then there is also an absence of demands in some other families. Seldom does a child encounter the opportunity of failing and learning from the mistake, because parents will condemn him totally, concentrating all their negative resources on the child's failure. We progress ignorantly to perceive only the innocent shortcomings of our children, never offering reassurance for their trying and attempting efforts. We, as parents learning through trial and error, are engaged in an irresponsible progress of destroying the incentives of our children. We have not conceived the possibility of understanding them, alienating our children because of our inability to comprehend, and the difficulty of enlightening ourselves with these flourishing times. We must conceive the reality that our children live in different eras, questioning our very own values. We must entertain undeniably a sense of tolerance in them and prevent them also from falling into cynicism and iconoclasm.

The second of the mainstreams where values are ascertained is the church, the ever reverent institution that implants moral values about life and death. Religion, offering spiritual profundity, shares intimately the distinct task of reaching society with remarkable prominence. The church, providing teachings about the creation of the world, man, and woman in Genesis and the Ten Commandments, offers the opportunity to repent, immaculately cleansing the soul of sin. The church provides Bible classes to acquaint our young children with Jesus and his teachings and the make them stronger against temptation and the evils of society. I would like to enlighten you, delicately releasing a formidable truth of singular propensity, with a powerful quote that says "a family the prays together stays together." The parents should evidently influence their children to attend church for spiritual help and peace from within, a difficult manipulation diagnosed to the astonishment of many. The church will teach Christ's basic attitudes about sex, marriage, adultery, homosexuality, and an undetermined number of problems that will torment people's lives. These teachings will unequivocally satisfy the fullest inquisitions of the mind, leaving an individual in some state of tranquility. The essence of the church is to consign people to Christ in recognition of the same authority and in the profession of the same faith. Children who are alienated from church assume credulously the biological theory of evolution as true, a concept that prevails in the public school system. The induction of this biological theory is the overwhelming thought that humans descended from a lower form of animal, a primitive principle that arouses strongly antagonistical sentiments in the church, and that through a long series of progressive modifications we evolved to our present status. Under certain conditions if becomes unconstitutional to teach from the Bible in the public schools, creating an imcomprehensible cloud that enhances gradually the alienation of Christ's teachings. This is why it is imperative to ensure a solid foundation for religion for our children, a resolution that should be of paramount importance to all. God is love and wisdom. One who has no religion has no God. One who does not have God is dangerous to himself and society.

The school is the third mainstream for acquiring extensive values about life and our form of government. So potent are the mandates of education that it necessitates that the children separate themselves for one-third of the day from their parents. This should immediately apprehend the parent's concern, arresting their attention on the various concepts infiltrating their children's minds.

Teachers eternally carry the heavy burden of serving as models to their students and, because of constant vigilance from everybody, should act accordingly. I, in pursuance of my vocation, have encountered several teachers who were seemingly unqualified in their endeavors as educators, a gross indiginity to the profession. A teacher is the instigator for the organization of thoughts, dispersing knowledge and inculcating a love of learning in children. Responsibility is the common denominator to achieve the essence and qualities of school and life. Education, an alienating wonder designed to stimulate the regions of the mind, provides new concepts, challenging theories, and ingenious inventions. I find it impossible to comprehend the insensibility of parents using the school system as a day-care center, never really grasping full possession of the significance of an education. Parents never become cognizant of their responsibility to provide incentives at home. It is demoralizing, basing my sentiments on solid facts, to see administrators and secretaries in air-conditioned offices while students and teachers are suffering in the classroom with an oscillating fan. Occasionally, a teacher and students will find themselves in the deporable situation of not even enjoying the luxury of employing a dilapidated fan. In regard to the matter of suggesting responsibility for permitting inadquacies in the schools, we must proceed, concluding with considerable truth, in finding the parents guilty of gross negligence, adjudicating them through the charges of ignorance. For my part I am convinced that parental involvement is the unique safeguard mechanism that will most definitely improve the quality of education for all the children. All in all, properly considered, schools do serve as a determinant of children's values, and parental involvement will stimulate the children with an enthusiastic admiration and determination, leaving them in a state of encouragement and absolute pleasantness.

Television, technology that has enhanced this generation's life beyond limits, is also an instrument manipulated to exploit the minds of people. Since there exists an unusual freedom from difficulty or effort to captivate an audience through television rather than books, predominately pupils in the school system, television magnates, and teachers are flirting with the irresistible concept of employing television as a method for teaching, devising the system with enthusiasm and without hesitation. Television, becoming a strong and sophisticated sensationalism, lacks self-criticism, requires reforming ideas, and stands in need of implementation for forecasting the truth without the uncontrollable desire of plagiarism. If in our simplicity we begin the challenging task of developing our children's values, hoping that our destiny will prevail, we need to be more critical of the programs they watch and be more suspicious of television. It is overwhelmingly understood that since the emergence of television, children have become, indeed, possessed by this magnificent discovery and obsessed with this wonder of the imagination. If we could teach our children to become more apprehensive about television, always in full possession of their faculties, mental and corporal, this would inevitably achieve the evidence of good judgment on their part, producing protective mental endowments for their benefit.

Friends, playing the ultimate major role of shaping the attitudes of young people, are like mirrors, reflecting an amiable philosophy among the collection of participants. Peer pressure, a dominant factor in influencing young minds, is a strong force that plays an unlimited role in molding negative and positivie habits. The influence that friends have on each other, mortifying some parents at their children's behavior, is so effective that we, under the circumstances, should plausibly pursue, striving with an optimistic purpose, the unfathomable course of teaching our children a sensible process of choosing compatible friends. It matters not how cautiously we object, dreading the inevitable events of the future; children will gradually follow the natural sequence of making their own decisions, choosing their own friends, and, most of all, learning from their mistakes, for something of this nature, allowing children to err and experience pain, is rewarding, providing that knowledge is incurred from the peculiarities of simply humanity. It is more than evident that we disapprove harshly of some of their friends, passing unfavorable judgment, condemning them easily, and capriciously refusing to comprehend and perceive the desperation we create in our children. Our guidance, based on a solid Christian faith, will help our children in life.

X
Strange Incidents

Sometimes, being cognizant of my overwhelming state of mind, I recollect some of the most shuddering and agonizing indicents revolving around my son's hideous tragedy. It arouses my senses and regains my memories when I, amid my infinite wretchedness, reminisce on foreordinations and posthumous happenings. The uttermost agony is one's inability to comprehend or decipher dreams, especially ones representing the destiny of an individual. Our faculties were irreproachable because of the impossibility to grasp what could have been friendly admonitions from the unconsciousness. I doubt it very seriously even if these incidents, presenting themselves as they did, had been celestial endeavors to enlighten our minds would have inspired immediate action on our part. We have not made ourselves available to spiritual insights. And these haunting incidents will live forever in my mind, harassing me in my thoughts, and tormenting me in my memories, day and night, whenever they enhance themselves relentlessly.

Precisely a week before Albert's calamity, Tina, my youngest daughter, made an appalling discovery of my pistol in the bureau of the bedroom. Apprehension, not to mention an inquisitive mind, impelled her to ask if the sudden impact and vibration encountered while slamming the drawer would consequently discharge the weapon instantaneously. There being no indication of danger, I, reading the newspaper assiduously and with great difficulty, managed to relieve her of the mental tension and anxiety.

I begged her to sit and focus her complete and undivided attention on a gloomy and horrible revelation I had just encountered. She read studiously and meticulously, deciphering and ascertaining facts on a suicidal story of a seventeen-year-boy. Of all my recollections, Tina had never before mentioned the gun in her life. Was this a warning, a sign of some unaccountable power? The circumstance was within human control, to apprehend the weapon, remove it from its existing locality, and place it in a more inconspicuous site. I now ponder upon this rare occasion. If I had exerted some concerned effort, would the course of history have been different? To me, this incomprehensible coincidence was, without a doubt and beyond the wildest configuration of my imagination, a divine warning of the catastrophe that was to unfold.

I never cease to think of Albert's two tragic automobile accidents, where he, with the grace of God, narrowly escaped death. It was a dismal gathering at the hospital subsequent to his second accident. The spirit was low, tension was high, and fear was the dominant atmosphere when I, through my verbal expression, related a noisome impression that perhaps, through the power of suggestion, might have penetrated his heart. I, positively and assuredly, ventured the noxious statement that he wouldn't have the satisfaction of surviving a future accident. The anomalous conditions induced me to expound such venomous and malignant words. The memory of it all is so depressing and distasteful. But the greatest of all the petulant pains was my premonition of Albert's death at a young and tender age. It was prognosticated through my dreams and thoughts. I had made my wife cognizant of my sense of foresightedness on several occasions. My sagacity had constantly disturbed me on account of my impetuous and profound insights. I tried unsuccessfully to banish this intolerable thought from the corners of my mind. Nevertheless, it persisted until resolving and materializing itself into reality.

Consider now the startling circumstance of an astonishing dream, introduced by my mother-in-law, giving the account of a rare phenomenon that anticipated death. Profoundly enough, thirty days before my son's death, conclusively and precisely to the time and day, his uncle Jimmy died. A week before Jimmy's death, his mother, my mother-in-law, dreamt of the apparition of her deceased husband, who died approximately ten years before, appearing to sequestrate one of their two sons. After it became apparent what his intentions were, she fought and struggled frantically to prevent him from accomplishing his mission. But in the vision, she could never, as considerably as she wanted to, discern the face of the son the father wanted to apprehend. It was seven days later that the youngest son, Jimmy, died. Days after the burial, I made an inadvertent remark to my wife, still lamenting her brother's death, that death comes in threes. Never did I perceive the possibility of Albert's death. This unforgettable remark still haunts me. Confessing the inability to comprehend will not alleviate or simplify my difficulty.

A few days after Albert's unbearable death, one disturbing night my wife was inevitably absorbed by a peculiar dream. To impress upon you the significance represented by this startling dream, I first have to acquaint you with the fact that my wife has never managed to possess the distinctive tendency of waking up during the course of the night to visit the children. This dream on this particular night was most unusual; some unknown force was beginning to make her feel uneasy. What was the ulterior motive of this dream? In her vision Albert was capriciously and vigorously violating her sleep, as if attempting to warn her vagariously of some immediate danger. He insisted vehemently, commanding her extreme consideration, never capitulating, never yielding, until reaching the overwhelming crescendo of infusing awakening qualities. Now in a state of consciousness, but still sullen with Albert's memory, she then proceeded to Tina's bedroom to unravel the mystery of the dream. Tina's bedlight, a yellowish light bulb, surrounded by floral organs such as petals, which give the deceiving impression of a flower head, had been covered or hooded inadvertently by Tina with a school jacket to dull the glare of the light. The jacket had initially started to smoke, gradually and steadily progressing to the perimeters of a pernicious fire, and nearly created another morbid and devasting situation. This phenomenal conveyance, perceived and apprehended by my wife's mental faculties, was a divine influence from the realm of God. Only God can ordain miracles far beyond human intelligence and attributes.

After the lapse of some weeks, Gina, our oldest daughter, found herself in a most peculiar situation, bringing to mind her brother Albert. While in a car as a passenger, just cruising around listening to the radio, Gina unexpectedly interrupted the music by changing the stations. And almost at the same instant, an iciness feeling possessed Gina's body while her thoughts reminisced on the numerous occasions when Albert had accompanied her. It may appear strange, but out of nowhere, Albert energetically shouted, *Gina, watch out!* Gina's attention was suddenly diverted to the road to realize that the friend, for no apparent motive or perhaps falling asleep behind the wheel, was driving off the road straight into an electrical pole. Gina hurriedly seized the steering wheel and swerved the automobile back on the road, avoiding an accident. Needless to say, Gina was quite confused and baffled by the unexplainable sensation, a paralysis that had struck her soul with a throng of memories of Albert.

Tina had established the capricious habit of vexing Albert for dwelling in the shower, bathing beyond the limits of time necessary for a normal person to achieve such a feat. A sense of anxiety would always sink in Albert. One night, about a week after Albert's death, all alone in the house, Tina was bathing, simultaneously recollecting the unrelenting occasions she would force Albert to tolerate her mischievous acts. As she was stepping into the hall, her eyes momentarily could not bring themselves to comprehend the image that beseiged them. For a few visible seconds she glanced at Albert, standing in the hall, glaring at her with a frown on his face, waiting impatiently for his turn to shower. There was no doubt of what she had just seen. It took her days to accumulate enough nerve to reveal the story because of the fear that we might deem her insane.

I have not been fortunate enough to experience such frenzied incidents as perceived by members of the family. The only recollection I have is concerning a picture Albert took three months before his death. Albert has posed for that picture in an artistic and upright position. His face, with a domineering look, projects a solemn appearance, characterized by an intent mental state. After Albert's death we succeeded in getting new impressions from this original picture. Upon receiving the reprints, my wife and I proceeded to satisfy ourselves by enjoying the new impressions, obtaining the great sensation we anticipated. It wasn't until a few seconds afterward, still meditating on the new impressions, that the distinct and most profound discovery concerning Albert's eyes was unfolded. The copies, by some inconceivable process, contrived the evidence and existence of tears, a phenomenon absent from the original picture. There was great uneasiness in our emotions. After I succeeded in recovering sufficiently from the state of delirium, I examined the pictures gingerly and with deliberation, missing no speckle from the face. It is therefore evident, beyond a shadow of a doubt, that the extraordinary facts speak for themselves. I was inclined to believe then, as I am now convinced absolutely, that this revelation was his way of saying, "I'm sorry, Mom and Dad."

Bringing to recollection all the different circumstances connected with Albert's death, the ultimate delineation of magnitude must be included to firmly convince others of the tremendous power our minds possess. It does not completely involve us, but indirectly reflects on our experiences and admonitions. A day after our calamity, Father Mitchell, expressing his devoted attention and exhorting us to be strong, visited our house. As we sat assembled in the front room, the initial conversation was about God and the latter part about admonitions of Albert. I was determined to convince Father Mitchell of my dreams, but he neither concurred nor rejected my acknowledgments. But with a remarkable and astonishing tale, it became evident that the latter part of our conversation was enhanced and deemed admissible by Father Mitchell. He recollected the tempestuous and turbulent occasion during the Vietnam War when he had the unfortunate task of notifying a particular family of their son's death. A colonel had accompanied Father Mitchell that sorrowful day. They resolved sagaciously to inform the soldier's father before directing their intentions to the mother. As both men coherently approached the soldier's father at his work they were discerned by him, an exhibition of gloom overshadowed the man. The colonel incisively vociferated the sad news, being as direct and thoughtful as possible, considering the shocking situation. The man acknowledged what is to some the inevitable conclusion of war. After fully absorbing the facts, also enduring the pain with a manlike aptitude, there ensued a most peculiar confession on his part. In his deep sorrow and melanchoy, he calmly revealed that he was already cognizant of his son's death. His voice, unbalanced and barely audible, proceeded to deteriorate as he continued to explain his wife's dreamlike vision foretelling their son's death. As the three men engineered their way to the mother's employment, making themselves visible to the faculties of the mother, she, in an agonizing and vociferous clamor, directing herself to the husband, said, "I told you he was dead; I told you he was dead." As tears poured down her eyes, her voice trembling excessively, still unbearably perplexed by the upsetting information, she gave account of the incredible dream she had on Thursday of the previous week. She sternly insisted that her son was killed on that day. The colonel injected with all due respect that her son was killed on Friday, not Thursday. Father Mitchell, listening to the whole proceedings attentively, generously reminded the colonel of the international date line. When it was Thursday in the United States, it was Friday in Vietnam. The mother continued, finding merely relating her story difficult because, in the midst of her dream, there was no discernable impression of her son's face. All she saw was his figure, his shadow fading away in her dream. Within two weeks after the conversation, overshadowed with impatience and anxiety, and upon arrival of the son's coffin, the mother demanded to unseal the casket. She regretfully terminated her curiosity respecting her son's faceless figure. His face had been obliterated by a bomb.

XI
Changes

Today, gradually overcoming the lapse of insensibility, awakening from the reveries of death, and reaching into the consolation of thoughts the mind must recollect, I am now cognizant of certain inane acts displayed by my son. These inanities escaped the ordinary powers of my mind and never whetted my mental energies to avert disaster. I was at the time a mere mortal without the ability to perceive the manifestation of gradual change in him, changes and conniptions vacillating between hope and despair.

My postmortem inquiry upon the consummation of my son's fate has led me with harassing thoughts to unearth numerous changes in his character. It harasses me because it haunts my mind, an occurrence that has been exacerbated lamentably during the course of this writing event. I have labored in earnest, and the compensation of my industry has evoked a series of indications that, in their consquences, brought destruction. My initial purpose is to place before you these indications and to indulge in my passion detailing the cause and effect of each. They are as follows:

1. quitting football
2. grades falling
3. skipping school
4. quitting school
5. loss of friends

6. changing sleeping habits
7. changing eating habits
8. running away from home
9. being involved in two car accidents
10. death of his closest uncle

My investigation, marked by thoughtful prudence and a careful analysis of the problem, rendered it evident that certain indications occurred within close and immediate intervals of each other. You must keep steadily in mind, clearing any impalapable shadows of the situation at hand, that extent of time undergone to unfold these unrelenting changes was in the vicinity of four years. My methodical examination, carefully and decisively observed, revealed emphatically that I deceived myself by not being critically perceptive of the road of doom my son was walking. I clearly missed the graduation of his actions, the origin that I speculated at the time was a typical revolutionary phase that besets young people in our society.

As I reminisce unboundedly on my son's school days, achieving immense information because of my insatiable greed to satisfy the constitution of my heart, I found that his membership in the football team inspired him with profound veneration during his brief school life. The ardent intensity that he cherished for the sport overpowered any evil temptations that emerged daily. I am being superfluous intentionally to succeed in my explaining endeavors of the nature of gratification the sport had upon my son. During the development of his youth, building an untainted character and achieving greatness on the field, he maintained academic excellence with a fit of enthusiastic interest. Then, in defiance of his own constitution, involving his own exploits, the complexity of his nature engendered. The ulterior motive, an unconquerable force that impels men, was the addition to a young lady. Falling prey to and enslaved by this ungovernable passion, his destiny with the football team had speedily encompassed complete failure. He had guided himself to an unsuccessful termination from the team with the mastery of his own actions.

The sense of falling from grace, a sudden disturbance that disappointed me without my being able to explain it, never occupied my mind, even with the complete powers of thought, as the initial development of the tempest that awaited us. Scarcely had I accommodated my mental faculties to his departure from the team, or better yet, developed a proper condition of mind for said departure when his school grades began to fall into a state of mediocrity. It was at this precise period, observing the prevailing behavior that flowed inconspicuously beyond my conception, that I should have inferred a vibratory revolution was occurring. My constant miscalculation of the whole situation, invariably buried in my mind, included a wide indeterminancy, never reaching my human habitat of reasoning or logic. Even my spirit peremptorily refused to embrace and decipher the meaning of the unpleasant mystification. I, so lucrative in education, so wealthy in knowledge, and so affluent in learning, was never competent to infiltrate the parsimonious thoughts of my son. What makes this tragedy unequivocally painful, flagrantly shocking, and submissively egregious is that I, so precise in observing people, failed with my son.

Still the changing deeds continued, loud and bold, more hideous each time, reaching a stage of depression and unveiling its shuddering destination. Soon after, while I was still regarding the whole matter lightly, his attendance in school became incessantly incorrigible. Immediately afterward, the whole situation so teemed and impressed with a setting of capriciousness, his own action induced the incredible emergence of removing himself from school. He approached me with a human effort befitting a man of eloquence, expressing himself with a quality of brilliance that would, in the avenue of the populace, make any father proud of his own son. From the inception of this touching circumstance, I was fervidly opposed to the concept vehemently, expressing intense objections, disrupting the serenity of the time without hesitation. And finally, victimized by his desirable goal, I became evidently influenced by his suggestion.

It didn't take long, watching the development with my appalled senses, before distinctive patterns of irregularities were rapidly unfolding, increasing with the affliction of anxiety. Albert's amiable nature, an innate disposition since the principal days of his youth, was beginning to flee momentarily. Days of turmoil began to rest steadfastly, gazing at him in the face, day after day, and setting in the bosom of his heart.

Disturbing the depths of my memory, the recollection of my thoughts comes throbbingly to mind with an agonizing sensation that makes my soul tremble. As time rolled along, ere long, his waywardness manifested itself in a rigorous seclusion, divorcing him from the throng of friends. This brief period of solitude, covering a rigid seclusion without apparent object, excluded the involvement of his young lady. She was his sole companion, his last love, before surrendering his life and reason together. For some time his friends grew more scattered, and his countenance had been, to a great degree, altered. There were futile attempts to combat his peculiar temperament, but the efforts were to no avail. There was an inconsistency on my part due to an irredeemable anger that pervaded my character.

Albert's changing demeanor, taking full possession of

his soul, was steady and persevering. His sleeping habits, the next startling phenomenon, became altogether most conspicious and unaccountable due to the sense of the situation. Lack of sleep, becoming impulsive in the extreme, was producing a peril to his health. A series of great impetuosities were the immediate consequences concerning himself and others.

The creeping change also managed to assault his eating habits, exhibiting a perceptible contamination on his handsome physique. Such beauty of body, suggesting excellence of form and qualities of dignity, was overshadowed by an unseemly loss of weight, which occasioned me great, great concern. I attempted with absolute precision, confronting a problem of undeniable depth, to relate a frightful picture, a graphic description in words of the inevitable fate that awaited him, hoping to inculcate fear for his subsequent condition. Through the tenacious efforts of my imagination, employing cultivated words in an adroit manner, success finally surfaced with so exquisite a precision. We had entered, enjoying the greatest feeling of confidence, a mutual arrangement susceptible of improvement.

As the days of our lives continued, taking advantage of this occasion to convey a happy medium affecting the whole family, our immediate discourse turned chiefly to mending this hazardous condition that had previously developed. I, being in good spirit and good health, busied myself once again with my own affairs, never thinking of the delicacy of Albert's position. I must say, contrary to much of the adverse and unfavorable sentiments vehemently verbalized, I was completely gratified and perfectly satisfied, expressing my entire appreciation with profound contentment. As I continue to reminisce, employing the ordinary powers of the mind, I remember that nothing of major consequence disturbed or interrupted the serenity of our domesticity. It was during this brief period of time, unquestionably the finest, for I am convinced with a definite impression of the time dimension, that I was preeminently blessed with the quality of a peaceful sleep. Prior to this dreary situation, as I endeavor to call it to mind, sleep was an experience nearly bordering the state of anxiety, rest always a matter almost out of the question. I knew, tantalized by the temporary intervention of perfect sensibleness, that this state of tranquility would never perpetuate itself.

My wife and I with the greatest exertion and with an extremely deep emotion, spent a significant part of our time consolidating our thoughts during the struggle, encouraging each other to endure the difficulties and dangers that encompassed us with our son. We searched for a long time, laboring without effect, for a remedy. Our attempts were unsuccessful and futile because Albert's inexplicable vicissitudes continued, as he constantly walked a disastrous path in life. Making matters still more distressing, with no indication of relief in sight, our son became influenced by some intimate associates of his, causing a solemn and grave disquietude in us. As I pondered upon some solutions, fighting desperately to alter his evening ventures with his friends, he became more absorbed in his amusing diversions. It was deemed proper for me to confront him, fearing that some serious adversity would befall him. When I anxiously approached him, questioning his unbecoming and unbending life-style, he received the criticism peevishly, expressing a look so dispirited. Today, when I embrace the collection of my thoughts, that indelible expression still haunts me, bringing sorrowful tears to my eyes and a never yielding pain to my heart. The inevitable result of this confrontation was his departure one night from home, rendering uneasy nights for us. It was exceedingly difficult to accept the fact that for two weeks our son disappeared, wandering around without even visiting us. The shock of his departure and the absence from home, which occasioned much suffering, occupied in our minds an uncertainty about his future. Subsequent to his departure, the family mood was affected radically, creating a sense of hope, a lingering eagerness for his return. That Christmas Eve, as I allude to the full possession of my graceful memories of my son, he came home. The ecstasy of his return overshadowed overwhelmingly the inquisition of the gross impropriety of his departure. I found the moment to be exceedingly pleasing. Reason and compassion influenced by natural sensations, implanting an everlasting bliss in the depths of my memories.

After the brief interval of a week, on New Year's Eve, as the force of the tempest that awaited us was still dormant, the whole family, being in a festive mood, was celebrating at my sister's house, anticipating midnight to discharge our firecrackers. While the sizable assembly of our family was in the midst of gaiety, it was at that precise moment that Albert and a friend of the family seized the initiative to depart from the festivity, their all-absorbing interest, an impetuous choice, apparently driving them hurriedly, was to purchase cigarettes. Back in the midst of the merriment, as the family reveled in their boisterous gathering and as the Almighty premeditated His following sequence of events, it was I that produced an inquisitve environment. My immediate apprehension of a rather startling situation prevented me from resuming in the convivial atmosphere. My curiosity respecting the inquisition consumed me with the consciousness of fear, a fear that pervaded my mental faculties with a deathlike feeling. Rising from the sofa, becoming irresistibly dizzy or, perhaps, confused and fearful of the potent effect of the unknown feeling, I immediately informed the family of my intention to search for Albert, resolving to rid my mind of the unpleasant and undesirable power that dominated my spirit. As I drove desperately in a state of confusion, exploring visible areas of the vicinity, my heart began to sink into a state of misery. Then an unaccountable circumstance, a mysterious effect of nature, penetrated my mind and body, forcing me and my vehicle to an undetermined site. My pensive mood during the quest, somewhat of a dreamy sensation, enhanced my divine belief that it was God, my co-pilot, guiding every arousing and stimulating action in my body. At this particular moment, upon arriving at the strange and unknown site, I recollected my senses instantaneously, as if awakening from a long, insensate dream. I, still drowsy from the power that had consumed me, advanced to a serious automobile accident that had arrested my unanimous attention. I dashed wildly to the scene, recognizing our friend's vehicle demolished in the mishap and with accelerated adrenaline and a pair of potent lungs, did not hesitate to scream my son's name. The exploration attempt to locate my son, finding courage in the midst of the desperation that environed me, led me to the frightful discovery that one of his legs was severely hurt and was in an undetermined condition. He had been transported, with extreme caution, from the violent scene to the hospital. I surged onward, although close to a state of convulsion, to our New Year's gathering, contemplating the mode of unfolding the details of the unfortunate development, as the agony of suspense on my son's condition increased insufferably. I recovered my composure long enough to inspire a process that afforded me the means of successfully relating the shuddering terror. I proceeded to breathe more freely, but the arresting tears and piercing screams of the family members brought to mind the undergone agony, forcing me to lapse into the previous state of insensibility. The entire atmosphere was marred by the wearisomeness of the accident, fracturing our son's right femur and ending the year in trying circumstances of wild desperation.

As the powers in my mind enable me to recall, the difficulty that transpired was definitely trivial, compared it to the second climax of despair that produced itself in facsimile. We had already entertained the concept that the initial accident encountered was too ghastly to repeat itself, suppressing that bitter, tantalizing taste of death into oblivion. A full memory with a past experience, confirming the worst thoughts of that dark event that oppressed us, successfully conditioned us for the intensity of another unpleasantness. Having barely survived the first peril that we dreaded horribly, this did not prove beneficial to our son. After two intense years, in spite of our thoughtfulness and serious devotion, showing interest and great solicitude, our complete attention was now diverted to yet another dreadful danger. The second catastrophe, heightened by a compound fracture to the same right femur previously injured, unmistakably protracted the deliverance of a healthy being. Amid those restless and sleepless nights, induced through our son's state of inactivity, another New Year's Eve prevailed upon us. Those weary nights, confounded by our son's inexplicable fate, resurrected an incongruous understanding of immeasurable depth, unraveling a fathomless compassion for his perpetual suffering.

Educing from my personal rudiments of life, penetrating what constitutes my philosophy of metaphysics, and through my analysis afforded by the number of his intricacies, I speculated that the tenacity of his tragic consistency presented the extenuating circumstances of being absolutely unnatural, as if some unknown external power had destined his idiosyncracies to be a series of painful experiences. The depth of my memories still holds bondage a certain irrepressible experience. While within the confines of the hospital, characterized with the qualities of an apathetic lethargy, I volunteered, deliberately and in jest, an effectual effort to smile, but he could not reciprocate. It was not his condition that rendered a smile useless, but his spirit that had been weakened by his fate.

There was never an ultimate recovery, as Albert adapted his stature to a limp, forever favoring his left leg. He managed to overcome his second negative occurrence of life, fully cognizant of the limited application of his condition. But time, the incessant clock of life itself, was running out, as fate was beginning to strike the exact hour. During the last month of his life, as the atmosphere of death was infiltrating the scene, there came an impact with the fury of despair that enhanced his tragedy, the climax that influenced the anguish of his fate and the catastrophic fulfillment of his destiny. The untimely death of his intimate uncle, destroying a profound attachment, produced an adamant effect in Albert, invincibly affecting his thoughts, nature, and behavior. The indescribable sensation took possession of his soul and mind, becoming the principal grief that riveted his attention unanimously. As I pen my memories, never will I forget the distressing mystery on his face. There was confusion in his heart, but the attention was on the dead, not the living. I did not apprehend the immediate danger that filled him with despair. Mental distress had overwhelmed him, disguising his feeling in silence throughout his uncle's funeral. It was this startling circumstance, exposing him to the natural consequences of death, that affected the unconsciousness, satisfying the natural curiosity of dying and absorbing the extraordinary attention occasioned by the trauma. Astonished by his uncle's incident and actuated by the ritual itself, the sanctity of his character started to dwindle into his fated circumstance.

At this present moment of my life, for some undetermined and peculiar reason, an absence of memory, a confusion of mind has paralyzed my mental faculties, depriving me of the recollection of my son's last days on earth. I have endeavored, in my extremity, remaining frantically perturbed at myself, to restore the loss of such precious memory. My negligence at the time has limited my struggle emphatically. In the midst of those unfortunate days, fate struck the hour of death, annihilating the consciousness of life for us. One day, God, the Infinite, through His mysterious ways will provide me the light to see in the dark.

XII
Conclusion

The consolidation of my thoughts, arranging the elements of my literature for the conclusion of the book, is in perfect unity, producing a much desired aesthetic effect. My sententiousness, expressed in pithy phrases to sermonize, propagates my agonizing story with impressions so painful in memories. Amid my dolorous misery, paralyzing the spirit, three years have elapsed since that ghastly tragedy, forcing me occasionally into an incoherence of the mind. It is an impossibility, far beyond the comprehension of human faculties, even to the most vigorous of all human imaginations, for you to feel my pain through any form of sententious writing. In the midst of all my infinite misery, I summon, from the depth of the immediate presence of my strength, a mountain of courage to communicate, conveying my innermost thoughts in a laconic style of expression and with the most luminous language possible in my vocabulary, in the trauma of unexpected discourse. Of all the omnifarious tortures in the world, diversifying them into distinctive categories, even falling into a condition of absolute agony, the totality of pain would still be inferior to that of losing a loved one. It is beyond the complete comprehension of any methodical attempt, regardless of the examination and analysis of the principles or methods of inquiry applied, to rectify my son's decision that fateful day. My arduous venture, challenging the confines of my thoughts with the intensity of my passions, excavating the remains of my lamentable circumstance, is one of personal experience. Because of my own ill-defined interpretation of death, never endowed with an understanding of the natural process of it and being influenced by the agonizing circumstance that environed me momentarily, consequently I contemplated death. In the totality of my endurance there was not a trace of physical pain, but of mental anguish an infinitude. Gradually, as time enervated my desire, I succeeded in recovering my resoluteness of will to survive, overcoming the embrace of death unanimously. I had concluded, characterized with the attribution of steadfast determination, even though irresistibly agitated in spirit, and notwithstanding the crisis, to persevere. In the solitude of my life I bedew my son's memory with my tears, exculpating him from his irreproachable fate. The conglomeration of facts, dictating the absolute necessity to substantiate my discourse, was inherited from a profound tragedy, a tragedy, nevertheless, that, incorrigibly distressing, may be beneficial to the multitude, willingly to consume the veracious proceedings of the subject narrated. Since the inception of this strenuous undertaking, radically affected by the bitter taste of death and analyzing the evidence through the whole period of its development, the principal objective was to arouse an appreciation of great magnitude and to awaken an effective channel of communication toward your loved ones, obliterating the capricious phenomenon of underrating them and infiltrating your heart with the love and attention they merit.

My writing enterprise, assuaging my emotional experience and mental perturbation minutely, has exhausted me. Some particular days, apprehensive at the approach of every morning, are long and weary, accompanied by the everlasting thoughts of my son. My spirits are convincingly dampened, and my heart is so thoroughly deadened, conclusively. I have busied myself with my tedious labor, forever camouflaging the sense of guilt that I must carry eternally in my heart. The ordinary powers of my mind were not fully prepared to expose what was conceived to be the nature of his affliction, unmasking my total failure in the capacity as father. Something of this nature, circumstances beyond my imagination, totally bewildered me, leaving my bosom full of indelible thoughts.

Those days when our son charmed us with the vivid splendor of his grace, when our hearts fancied the spirit of his youth and our love caressed the livelihood of his existence, are now entombed in the grave of our memories, echoing exclusively the vibration of our thoughts. As I anticipate gracefully the evening of my life, I find substantial credibility, because of my faith, in the destiny of a rendezvous, in life after death, with my son. And when my sun sets, darkening the vision of my eyes and descending below the horizon of my life, my immortal soul, the principle of life in me, will ascend to the Kingdom of our Supreme Being. There in Heaven, the house of God and His angels, in the midst of that holy sanctuary, where souls become consecrated, I will initiate, in that extremely sacred paradise, sanctified by God, in that hallowed garden of Eden, a state of supreme bliss, the quest for my son. And when I find him, after all those passing years that have elapsed, I will eagerly embrace him in the bosom of my heart, the seat of my emotions. There he will dwell with me, in the embrace of my arms, where he will never die again.

Son, forgive me.